AMERICAN BEAUTY

AMERICAN BEAUTY

THOM FILICIA

Photographs by Eric Piasecki

CLARKSON POTTER/PUBLISHERS

NEW YORK

Published in the United States by Clarkson Potter/Publishers,
an imprint of the Crown Publishing Group, a division of Random
House, Inc., New York.
www.crownpublishing.com
www.clarksonpotter.com

CLARKSON POTTER is a trademark and POTTER with
colophon is a registered trademark of Random House, Inc.

Library of Congress Cataloging-in-Publication Data
Filicia, Thom.
    American Beauty / Thom Filicia. — First edition.
    1. Filicia, Thom—Homes and haunts—New York (State)—
Skaneateles.   2. Interior decoration—Philosophy.   I. Title.
    NK2004.3.F55A35   2012
747—dc23   2011052490

ISBN 978-0-307-88490-9

Printed in China

Design by Stephanie Huntwork

10 9 8 7 6 5 4 3 2 1

First Edition

TO ALL MY FRIENDS AND NEIGHBORS
IN SKANEATELES WHO MAKE IT SUCH A
WONDERFUL PLACE TO CALL HOME

CONTENTS

FOREWORD 8

INTRODUCTION: HOW I BOUGHT A HOUSE
IN A PLACE CALLED HOME 10

1 THE HOUSE INSIDE MY HEAD 25

2 REINVENTING THE HOME 41

3 THE ESSENTIAL ELEMENTS 63

4 THE LIBRARIAN LETS DOWN HER HAIR 87

5 PUTTING IT ALL TOGETHER 101

6 LETTING A HOUSE BE A HOME 205

EPILOGUE 216
ACKNOWLEDGMENTS 219
RESOURCES 220

FOREWORD

Hello. When I read Thom Filicia's first book, *Style,* I fell in love with his way of designing interiors. I had been a fan of Thom's since *Queer Eye,* and had harassed him at more than one NBC party, but seeing his work unfettered by the extreme time and budget constraints of reality TV, I was really impressed with his legit training, his visual style, and his ability to translate his philosophy into practical tips for nerds. I really wanted to work with him. His rooms were warm, earthy, fun, and a little bit masculine—just like me!

I was determined. If I was ever going to leverage this temporary TV celebrity of mine, it would be to get Thom Filicia Inc. to design my family's apartment. Of course it turns out that you don't have to be on TV to collaborate with TFI, and a meeting was easily arranged to discuss the project. When we met, I asked Thom to autograph my copy of his book. (I should point out that I never ask anyone for an autograph, and I have met Paul McCartney and Posh Spice.) My husband and I enjoyed our collaboration with Thom immensely and continue to marvel at our good fortune when we look around our lovely grown-up home.

In *American Beauty,* Thom tells the story of saving and renovating an old house, but it seems to me it's also a story about going home again and loving your hometown. (Who knew Thom grew up near a town with a polo club? Classy.) It's an appreciation of a pre-homogenized America, when each state and town had its own look and feel. It's a book that offers great pragmatic advice. But it's also the perfect book for when you want to lock yourself in the bathroom, hide from your children, and look at pretty pictures.

Once signed, this foreword is a legally binding document that states that Thom must help my family with any home we live in until the end of time.

Sincerely,

TINA FEY
NEW YORK CITY

HOW I BOUGHT A HOUSE IN A PLACE CALLED HOME

BEFORE I BECAME THOM FILICIA—BEFORE I BECAME KNOWN AS ONE of the "Fab Five" on a TV show called *Queer Eye for the Straight Guy,* before I had an interior-design firm with my name on the door, before my years of apprenticeship at the legendary design house Parish-Hadley—I was Tommy Filicia, a kid from Syracuse. I grew up in a neighborhood of the city called Sedgwick Farm, a stately old collection of houses built in the 1920s around a club where tennis whites are still required. I then moved up the hill to study design at Syracuse University. Although some of my old Sedgwick crowd has drifted away from our hometown, mostly to New York City, when we meet, for dinner or by happenstance on the street, it's like running into an old friend from summer camp.

Quakers organized a local society in 1812... Just before the Civil War, they maintained two houses in the village... stations of the "underground railway"... aiding slaves to reach Canada safely...

Roman Catholic Church St. Mary's of the [...] first services [...]

STREET

BUILDINGS PICTURED BELOW
① Methodist Church - organized 1832.. Building erected 18[..]

EAST
② Baptist Church, organized 1832.. Building erected [...]
③ Grange Hall No. 458
④ Skaneateles Lodge #522 F.&A.M. chartered June 12, 1862

ACADEMY

FIRE HOUSE

Sto[...] Built [...] John [...]

Sherwood [...] original built [...] 1805

STATE STREET

Skaneateles Library Building erected 1880

Built [...] prominent [...] home of the [...]

EAST GENESEE

[...] STREET

Lutheran Holy Trinity Church founded 1913

First Skaneateles private yacht... a 40 foot sail-boat built for Col. Vredenburgh in 1812.

Episcopal Church [...]

Skaneateles Lake

LAKE STREET

WEST

Skaneateles has all-American charm that draws shoppers, bicyclers, and Sunday drivers on summer days. The residential streets in the village are lined with Victorian-era Italianate and Federal houses. Sitting on an old-fashioned front porch, looking out on shady sidewalks and bustling streets, you can watch the world go by.

My friends from home are usually surprised to hear that I go back regularly and still hang out with people they haven't seen in years. I make the four-hour drive to attend weddings, to celebrate the birth of friends' babies, or to see my father, who recently moved to Skaneateles for the summer. For the previous few years, as I appeared more often on television, the people who used to call me Tommy have wanted me to show up as Thom at fund-raisers, where my little bit of renown might bring more locals out and put a few more dollars into the hat.

That's what I was doing in the quaint lakeside town of Skaneateles, about forty minutes southwest of Syracuse, on a gorgeous afternoon in the middle of July 2008. I had spent the day at a benefit for the Syracuse Opera held at the Skaneateles Polo Club. Standing at the head of one of the Finger Lakes—the long, narrow, high-country lakes that central New York is famous for—Skaneateles is a place that time (and chain stores) seem to have forgotten, yet it's a modern, lively town with its own small airport, cute shops, a prosperous vineyard, and marvelous restaurants. I had been coming to Skaneateles since I was a kid, first to swim and fish with my childhood friend Robbie and later to hang out with my high-school crew—Robbie, J.R., and Ben, whose father owned the Sherwood Inn, a historic hotel and restaurant overlooking the lake. When we were sixteen or so, we would slip beers out of the Sherwood's coolers and sneak back to a friend's boathouse for a party.

Even if I didn't have a history there, I would still feel at home in Skaneateles. Its streets are lined with clapboard Colonial-, Italianate-, and Victorian-style houses. The locals stop to chat as they come and go from the shops. It's a place that loves its traditions. Every spring the whole town is on hand for high-school graduation in Shotwell Park, across from the Sherwood—after which the new graduates make their traditional dash into the lake in their gowns. In summertime the population seems to double every weekend. But if you hang around the bar at the Sherwood long enough, you'll eventually see anyone in town you're looking for—or at least get the scuttlebutt about what he or she has been up to.

The auction at the country club was a typical Skaneateles event: far from being a stuffy old institution, the opera is a spunky, upstart company that many of the younger Syracuse families who retreat to Skaneateles in summer support; the polo club is also a place where the whole community gathers. I spent the day running the auction with Carrie, my pal who is a local TV personality—I call her Syracuse's own Katie Couric. We had a grand time and along the way made some bucks for a good cause, reconnecting with some people and meeting others, and we left with a few fun stories to tell.

Late that afternoon, heading back to Manhattan, I had just started along the east side of the lake when I spotted a for-sale sign on the right side of the road. I had driven this stretch not a month earlier and hadn't noticed the sign then. Of course, I wasn't looking for a house—at least I didn't think I was: before I knew what I was doing, I had pulled over and was craning my neck to catch sight of what they were selling.

OPPOSITE: The house, viewed from the lake. **ABOVE**: The lake cruiser *Judge Ben Wiles.* Its sister craft, the *Barbara S. Wiles,* delivers mail along the lake all summer. **RIGHT, ABOVE AND BELOW**: My Chris-Craft was one of the first personal items I brought over from my old lake house.

I couldn't see the house clearly from the road. It stood shrouded in trees at the bottom of a deep lot that sloped from the mailbox to the water's edge. Whatever was down there had lots of yard—and lots of privacy. Its location on the lake was also perfect. I had driven about a mile and a half out of town. Whether you went by road or by boat, the house was close enough to town to make shopping or an impromptu dinner out convenient. But it was far enough away from the lake's end that it probably had a wide-open view across the water.

The truth was, I didn't need a new house. I already owned one on a lake in eastern New York State, a lot closer to my home and business in Manhattan. I didn't have the time to get involved in a project more than four hours upstate. With the economy already showing signs of tanking, it didn't make any sense to put a significant amount of money into a house that I would visit only on the odd weekends I could get away. Still . . . Maybe it was the fun I'd had that afternoon, or the pull of home, but despite all the reasons to drive on, I thought, *What's the harm in looking?*

I backed up and turned into the driveway. As the house came into view, I could see it had suffered years of benign neglect. The brown siding badly needed new stain. The roof was intact but tired. To the right of the front door on the ground floor, a window was completely blocked by the trunk of an enormous maple tree. There was a large, separate garage with kooky nautical windows, but I'd hesitate to park even an insured vehicle there. The house's basic design was nothing spectacular—it might be described as a Colonial, but with its brown cedar siding and sloping roof, it had the feeling of one of the original camp houses the first summer visitors built on the lake in the late 1800s.

I was a little bit relieved—a place in this shape might actually be a bit more affordable—and a little dismayed: I had no reason to turn right around and drive off. The house was neither too grand nor too broken down. It had possibilities.

Somebody was circling around the lawn on a little John Deere. When he spotted me, he turned off his mower and came over to introduce himself as Howard, the caretaker of the property. Howard didn't offer to let me in, but he let me look around outside all I liked. When I walked around back, I saw that the lake side was the true front of the house: symmetrical, with a peaked roof on either side. A low-slung charm overcame its poor condition.

More important, it was perfectly placed on the lot, nearly square to the shoreline, well away from the road, and a short walk to the water, ending a couple of stepping-stones into the lake. The views were just as I had imagined. Across the lake, a red barn and silo sat at the top of a grassy rise. Below them, elegant houses from various periods dotted the shore.

Looking back, I suppose it was inevitable that I would end up owning a house in a place like Skaneateles. I'd grown up on lakes like Oneida, where my family kept a classic Penn Yan cruiser. Summer had always meant zipping across a lake on a sailboat, or water-skiing, or running out the back door for a swim with friends. I love the ocean and have enjoyed every

Pricing a Fixer-Upper

WHEN CONSIDERING THE RIGHT PRICE for a home, estimate the cost of the improvements that you'll have to make and those you'll want to make. If you don't know how to estimate this cost, ask a contractor or an experienced home owner to walk through the house with you. Add this estimate to the price of the house. This figure represents the minimum amount you'd have to sell the house for to recoup your investment. A house selling for $500,000 that needs $250,000 worth of upgrades to make you happy living there will have to sell for at least $750,000.

Now look around the neighborhood. Are any houses comparable to yours selling for more than $750,000? If the cost of the renovation added to the purchase price goes beyond what a house can sell for, the house is probably not a great buy. (Or you need to scale back your standards.)

This is true even if, like me, you'd never think of flipping the place. I take as much pleasure in what's practical as in what's beautiful. If the recent real-estate crash taught us one thing, it's that there's nothing practical or beautiful about a house you can't get your money out of.

TOP: The house as it was the day I first saw it in the summer of 2008. The clapboard siding was badly weathered and the windows were a hodgepodge of styles. LEFT: To my surprise, the house was structurally sound. The changes needed to breathe life into the place were mostly cosmetic—and commonsensical.

minute I've spent at my brother's house and my summer rentals in the Hamptons. But when I was at last ready to buy a getaway of my own, I looked inward and decided the Hamptons wouldn't do it for me. I went looking for a lake.

About ten years ago, I bought a house on Copake Lake in eastern New York. No more than a mile square, Copake lies just south of the Berkshires, about two hours from Manhattan—close enough so that I could invite colleagues, neighbors, and city friends. For a long while, it was all I needed. As time went by, though, and I began to make my trips back to Syracuse, I realized it wasn't just any lake I wanted; I missed the Finger Lakes. They have their own culture

and their own mind-set: all lakes are not alike. I wanted one that felt like home.

My personal life wasn't the only thing that had been straying back toward central New York; the region had become a muse for my design ideas, too. About a year and a half before I encountered the house, I had begun working on my own furniture collection with a family-owned company from Hickory, North Carolina, called Vanguard. First I designed a dining chair based on the ancient *klismos*—the low, broad chairs with curving legs that you see on ancient Greek urns (and which have inspired many designers). Each piece in the collection was supposed to have a name, and I wanted to avoid generic pomposities like "The Harrington" or "Avedon." As I was contemplating all this, I happened to drive past a sign for Greek Peak, a ski area I used to frequent as a kid. I named my American version of the klismos the Greek Peak chair.

I began to give the pieces I added to the collection not just central New York names but real connections to the region. I'd find inspiration for my designs in a place-name or the childhood associations I had with a town or a building. Sometimes I would draw an idea for a color or a texture from a stone wall I saw in passing, and the area or farm where I'd seen it would end up as the name. Solvay, a town on Onondaga Lake, northwest of Syracuse, once famous for manufacturing steel and electric wire, inspired a swirling metal spot table. My sleek Weedsport chair reminded me of a race-car seat, so I named it after a speedway near Auburn, a few minutes' drive west of Skaneateles.

Some of the associations were more abstract. When it came time to design a dining table, I knew I wanted something classic, but with an element of cool sophistication. I arrived at a circular design with a metal base that would give the table a little edge. I had stopped

in the tiny village of Borodino and discovered a new gourmet food market set up in a former church. The sophisticated edibles like truffle sea salt and organic vegetables, displayed in the old church's classic setting, captured the same rediscovery of central New York that I was putting into my collection. I named my new table Borodino. By the time I finished the collection two years later, nearly every piece had been named after a town, a street, or a community within an hour's drive of Syracuse.

These shapes and materials and associations were more fundamental to me than anything I'd drawn from before. Instead of designing intellectually, using the principles of the masters I drew inspiration from, I rooted the furniture in the landscape and the architecture that surrounded me growing up. The furniture came from me because it came from the place I called home.

I was still figuring all this out when I first drove past the house in Skaneateles. Like my furniture designs, the house belonged to the landscape: it was fitted to its environment— open to the lake, bunkered against cold nights, made of wood and stone taken from its surroundings. Its lakeside camp style was completely of its time and place, too. It was modest enough to be a casual spot for parties with friends, yet I could make it as sophisticated as I wanted it to be. It fit *me*—a kid from Syracuse who wanted a place near home; a designer who was searching for an organic, personal style.

The next time I was in Skaneateles, I walked through the house. I knew in my gut that I was supposed to own this house. If I

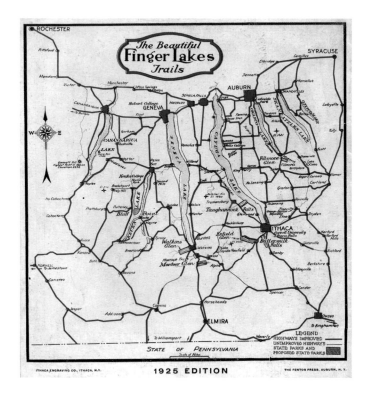

listened to logic, I knew I wouldn't buy it, but before I left that day, I told the real-estate broker, Ellen, that I wanted to make a serious offer.

Ellen had another idea: a lowball offer. When she named the figure she had in mind, I said, "Ellen, they'll never talk to me again."

But the owner did, saying no at first but starting a negotiation. One evening soon after we'd made our final offer, I was at the bar at the Sherwood Inn with my father and brother when I spotted Howard the caretaker. I went over to say hello. "I don't know what's going to happen with the house," I told him, "but if it works out, I'd love for you to stay on to help me."

A guy standing next to Howard turned and asked, "Which house is that?"

"Your house," Howard told the stranger.

Howard introduced us to Russ, the owner of the house. I immediately apologized about the lowball offer and Russ laughed. He told us the history of the house: how his parents had lived there. Then, thanks to my father and Russ, the conversation quickly turned to Cornell football. When it was time to go, I shook Russ's hand and told him, "However it works out, I love the house. I promise I'm not going to knock it down."

After we left, Howard told me later, he and Russ went directly from the Sherwood to the house, pulled the for-sale sign out of the ground, and threw it in the garage. "That's it," Russ told Howard. "That's who's getting the house."

A Brief History of Skaneateles

SIXTEEN MILES LONG AND A MILE and a half wide, Skaneateles Lake is surrounded by farms except at its northern end, where you find the town of Skaneateles and its 2,500 residents (plus summer visitors). The town has a well-developed sense of how to live. There is good food, annual wine and music festivals, and a triathlon. Between the busy schedule at the country club and community events, you could find a reason to be out and about every night.

At the same time, Skaneateles feels quiet—a little midwestern, even. The sensibility is old-school: the kids who come out to meet your boat at the marina and work in the stores downtown are polite. When you go out, there's parking! You know everybody in the restaurant or the grocery store or the liquor store. If you don't have your wallet with you, you take what you need and pay the next time.

The first vacation houses along the lake went up in the 1880s, when Syracusans took the trolley from the city. When automobiles became popular in the early twentieth century, the trip got easier: families could bring everything they needed for a weekend's stay, and drive it right up to their house. Prosperous farmers and mill owners sold land to prosperous New Yorkers. Teddy Roosevelt's brother bought a palatial white Georgian house that still stands on a rise on the west side of the lake.

My house was a product of this initial burst of construction. Built in 1917, it stood on a parcel of land bought from the Shotwells, a wealthy family who had come to Skaneateles in the 1850s to open a mill and farm.

By the 1950s, Skaneateles was a well-known Finger Lakes destination, and its fame had spread beyond central New York. The Krebs, a restaurant known for its "home" cooking, drew movie stars and other bigwigs, like Eleanor Roosevelt. Older folks in town say they could go all the way to California and people would know Skaneateles for "that restaurant everyone talks about."

The prices for houses on the lake had been going up for years, even as Skaneateles remained a sleepy town known mostly to locals. Then, in the mid-1990s, Bill and Hillary Clinton spent a week's vacation on the lake and Skaneateles made the national news. Soon afterward, the lake began to draw people from Manhattan and Boston in addition to Syracusans and western New Yorkers.

< 1 >
THE HOUSE
INSIDE MY HEAD

NOT LONG AGO MY CONTRACTOR, DAVID LEE, WAS TELLING THE story of the day I came to his office to sign off on his proposal for the work. David is a practical kind of guy, as you might expect from a house builder, and that morning he had been planning on talking through some of the details of the upcoming demolition phase with me and his lieutenants, Alan and Jimmy. "Thom comes in and is talking about what paint color he's going to put on which walls," David recalled. "Thom was always looking so far ahead."

Don't tell David, but it gets worse than that. By the time he and I agreed to work together, I had plotted out for the most part where the furniture would go. I knew the window treatments I would use, and I was thinking about the art that would go on the walls. Maybe,

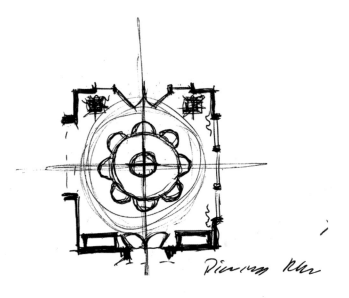

Dining Rm

Evening food.

as a designer, I think further ahead than most. But I don't recommend that anyone wait for the construction to begin before thinking about how the hardscape of the house will work with the soft furnishings. If you make the restoration and the interior design separate processes, they are bound to clash, or else you'll find out what you really wanted after it's too late to make changes to the house. When David, Alan, Jimmy, and the crew showed up for the first day of work on the house, they were making a start toward a picture of a finished design I had been carrying in my head for months.

My scheme for the house had really started the same day I had stumbled on it. On my drive back to Manhattan, I tried to dismiss the house from my mind, but I hadn't gone an hour before calling my friend Shauna. My mother had worked with Shauna's father in a real-estate office in Syracuse, and he now had his own firm, with Shauna as one of his agents. Shauna

put me in touch with her colleague Ellen, who promised to send me interior photos. They arrived in my office just as I was heading to the West Coast to visit an ongoing project.

On the flight home from California, I pulled out the photographs. They showed the expected elements of a lakeside camp: chunky, rough wood doors and dark-stained wood paneling. Though the rooms were nicely placed, with their longer walls facing the lake, they were divided by doors and unnecessary walls. The windows were small and oddly placed. The house didn't exactly make the most of the magnificent body of water outside its windows.

With a notebook in front of me on the tray table, I began to sketch out a floor plan so I could start playing with ways to open up the

My original sketches for the dining room and lake side elevation were made on a plane ride from California before I even owned the house.

house. A butler's door between the kitchen and dining room could come out. I'm not found in the kitchen too often (other than to grab mixers), and I have never burst through the kitchen door to present a roast on a platter to my waiting guests. My partner, Greg, who is an amazing cook and prepares fabulous meals for our guests, prefers to interact with our company while he's cooking, so I opened up the kitchen, X-ing out a redundant exterior door—it was just five steps from the front door!—and replacing the small, off-center window looking out to the road with a bigger one that was centered properly on the wall.

On the opposite end of the living room was a screened-in porch that looked as if it were about to fall down. This porch contained the sole door from the back of the house out to the lake, as well as a jumble of jury-rigged windows. Two of its walls were composed of raw logs, which was probably the house's original exterior siding. Enclosed and converted to year-round space, the room would make a counterpoint to the dining room.

Behind this threesome up front—dining room, living room, and screened-in porch—were two small bedrooms separated by a bath. This run of small rooms, I saw, could be turned into a miniature suite when family came to visit: a guest bedroom, a bathroom, and a small living room, with doors at either end for privacy. When it was unoccupied, the bathroom would serve as a powder room and the small living room would be the media room.

David Lee (far right) and I, with plans in hand, gather at the shoreline with the team to get some perspective on a decision we're trying to make. Though I had a detailed vision for the house, any project this big becomes a collaboration with the contractor. David and his guys were always there to help me work through the fine points of the plans.

The new overhang sheltering the front door
adds presence to the driveway entrance.

Adding Dimension

FIXING A FLAT
The house's biggest problem was that it was flat—it lacked dimension and punch. The roof came down low, making up a major part of what you saw from the driveway. The cedar siding was not ideal, but it was clean and crisp, so I could live with it. Here's how I added some pop to the exterior.

ENTRY Making a bigger deal of your front entrance is the fastest way to add visual impact to your house. I bumped out the entrance three feet to give it more prominence and to provide a better transition from inside to outside. It also created more room inside for the stairwell and its landings, which felt really narrow. At the same time I centered the window above the front door to give the entry even more visual heft.

ROOF The old roof had no leaks, but the asphalt shingles looked worn-out and sad. Originally I wanted to replace the siding with cedar shingles—which have great texture, and weather to a lovely gray patina—but in the end I opted to keep the siding and put shingles on the roof, dressed up with black, standing seam metal.

WINDOWS Windows, they say, are the eyes of a house. So why not put some eyeliner on for some pop? You want this effect to be subtle, so I chose windows with black frames, which make them stand out against the siding. To add even more depth, I combined the black with sashes that are a lighter shade, close to graphite. The two colors keep the effect lighter than if I had used all black. It also gives them a more custom, refined look.

BACKGROUND Even if the siding wasn't a horrible rustic brown it would have needed freshening. I painted it Knight's Armor, a color from Pittsburgh Paints, whose eco-friendly paints were used inside and out. Now it has a crisp finish that made the clapboard very appealing.

PEAKED ROOFS One thing that attracted me to the house was its classical symmetry. On the lake side were two peaked roofs at either end of the house, one over the dining room and one over the sunroom. I saw them as unornamented pediments— the triangular features you see above the entrance on ancient Greek or Roman buildings. All they needed was more presence. At the top of each pediment I added a few inches to the overhang, pulling the edge forward like the brim of a hat. At the bottom, I had David Lee trim off what I called "dog ears"—vertical pieces inserted in the eaves that cluttered the pediment shape. Then I added three architectural brackets to each side, in a shape I'd seen on a few older houses around Skaneateles. Finally, I hung a lantern inside each pediment, the same ones from Restoration Hardware that hang on either side of the fireplace inside. It's nice to return from dinner on the boat on summer nights and be welcomed by their symmetrical glow.

The second floor was dominated by the master bedroom that overlooked the lake. Abnormally long, the master may have begun as two rooms when the house was built that were later combined into one. The room's odd length was an opportunity to create another self-enclosed space, as I had done on the first floor, this time for myself. I drew a line across the room, dividing it into two sections. One took up about a third of the space, enough for an ample bathroom area containing a shower, a double-sink vanity, and a separate toilet room that I carved out by taking a small portion of the bathroom from the bedroom next door. The remaining two-thirds was now a normally proportioned rectangular bedroom. Two walk-in closets on the northern wall needed only a coat of paint and new hardware to be ready to house all my country couture. The other rooms upstairs—a bedroom and a small windowless

sewing room with great built-in linen storage— completed the self-sufficient upper floor: the second bedroom would serve as an office when I didn't need it for guests, and the sewing room would accommodate my washer and dryer.

The biggest change in the floor plan was the entrance. When I had approached the house the week before, I had been struck by how unassuming the place looked to anyone coming up the drive. It definitely needed an infusion of charm. Reviewing the real-estate agent's photos of the interior, I saw that the entryway, where most guests would first encounter the

OPPOSITE: The media room is joined to the powder room and the downstairs guest room by means of the hall, visible through the door at right in this photo. These three rooms can be closed off to form a small guest suite for families, with two bathrooms and with this sofa offering additional sleeping space for children.

interior, was tiny, an eight-by-five or so rectangle crammed under the stairs. On my floor plan I expanded this area, moving the front door out three feet and doing the same to the landing on the stairway directly above, which I see as a critical transition space between the first and second floors. The extra square footage would allow me to add more dimension to the space.

By pushing out three feet on the first and second floors, I had also created a focal point around the front door. An overhang over the front step and a set of tall windows on the second floor would give this entrance even more heft visually, making the house look more inviting to someone driving up to the front.

When I walked through the house for the first time with Ellen, my real-estate agent, a couple of weeks later, I could practically see the rooms as I'd drawn them up on my floor plan. The condition of the place, though, was worse

than the photos had shown. The kitchen was tragic—out-of-date doesn't begin to describe it—with well-used cabinets and counters and three layers of carpet on the floor. You didn't have to be an engineer to know that more problems lurked inside the walls. It would need everything—insulation, electrical system, plumbing, and a good set of squirrel traps.

Most curious of all were the windows, which were small and oddly placed. In the dining room, a bank of three windows faced the dimly lit side yard while a single, insufficient double-hung peered out at the lake. Dead center in the living room's lake-side wall was a bow window that looked like an emergency trans-

The evolution of the driveway entry as I extended the entry hall and stair landing above it three feet outward and added a welcoming peaked overhang with brackets.

plant from a 1950s split-level, flanked by small double-hung windows. The rest of the wall facing the lake was solid.

As Ellen talked me through the house, I was distracted by how dark the lake side was. I could almost hear a voice begging me to let the light in. Where the sad bow window was I imagined floor-to-ceiling windows. In the dining room and in the room that would replace the screened-in porch, I conjured up double sets of French doors that would provide bountiful light and access to the lake from anywhere you could see water. In the summer, the doors would stay open throughout the day.

Looking again, I put my line of new windows at the outermost point of the bow, not even with the existing living room wall. Now I would have a squared-off niche the height of the room and twelve feet wide. In that niche I pictured a sofa. To fill the space I would need a nonstandard size: nine feet long (leaving room for lamp tables at either end) and low enough, no more than twenty-eight inches high, so it would not block the windows or the view of the lake behind it. I saw a few friends sitting on it, silhouetted against the lake on a summer evening—check that, make it early fall, still warm enough to

Light pours into the living room through the five-window-wide niche that replaced the old bow window. The beams on the ceiling reinforce the room's visual thrust toward the lake, invisible here on a snowbound day. As soon as I had designed this niche, I drew up the sofa that would occupy it, which in turn donated its architectural *X* to the other ceilings in the house.

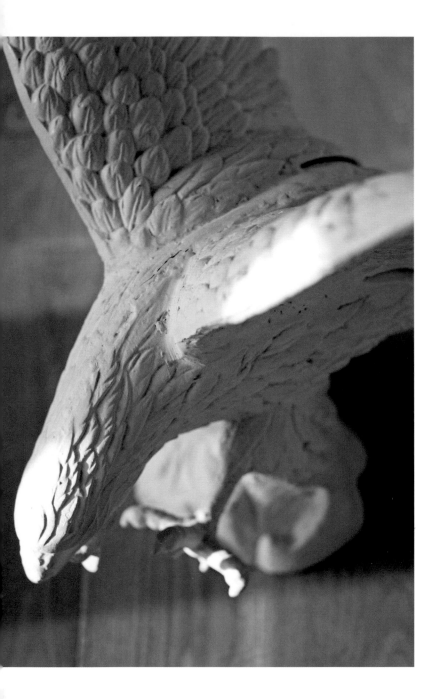

have the windows open, but with a fire roaring in the fireplace opposite.

When I sat down to sketch it, I gave the sofa a deep, flat seat with an arm that had a nice little slope to it. The shape was necessary to fit the requirements of the space, but I also liked its modern elegance; it reminded me of something by the midcentury furniture maker Dunbar. To pull it back a little toward the traditional, I put a low *X*-shaped stretcher on its base, inspired by the horse farms I drove past on my way up to the lake. Now the sofa looked like the house itself: traditional, with a modern simplicity and openness, and a design that tied the piece to its surroundings.

Many people think that the design of a house is like an assembly line, where all the pieces are added in chronological order: first the structure, then the paint, tile, and flooring, then the "soft" furnishings. For me, a decor can take shape either way along that timeline: a decision about materials for the floors, or an exposed beam can be influenced by my choice of a wall covering or a fabric—or a sofa. That *X* made its leap, for instance, from the sofa to the ceilings throughout the house. As I was sketching out my plan for the stairway, I realized that the ceiling there would be too low to hang a pendant or a chandelier. I didn't want to leave it completely undecorated, though, so I sketched in an *X*—the same slightly flattened version that braced the base of the Skaneateles sofa. Soon it became the default where there were no beams and the ceiling would otherwise be without texture.

Renovate or Obliterate

RENOVATION WORK IS ONE OF DAVID Lee & Company's specialties, and David likes to take a building that's on the verge of demise and bring it back to life. My house wasn't a worst case, but here are five guidelines I use to help decide whether to fix up any house or start over.

1. Does it have character and redeeming value? My house wasn't a museum piece, but there were certainly elements that made it worth saving, and I had a vision for how to preserve and enhance those elements. As you look at the house from the lakeside, you could see the original symmetry of the design. The twin peaked roofs added a lot of character, and the peak on the south side had a vaulted ceiling.

2. Is the house in the right spot? The house may be in the wrong place or at the wrong angle to give you the best views, which bolsters the argument for tearing it down if the house is also in disrepair. Be careful, though, if you have waterfront property. Zoning laws often dictate how close to the water a new structure can be built. If building from scratch means moving inland and losing connection with the water, it's probably better to renovate. In my case, the house was nicely situated on the lot, and nothing was to be gained by tearing down and relocating the structure.

3. What's the condition of the foundation? Cracked, uninsulated, or nonexistent foundations can create misery for a home owner, and no matter how nicely you renovate, foundation woes can inhibit the value of your house. If the problems are fixable, take care of them right away; no home owner is going to go back and do it later. The foundation on my house was wet but structurally sound. David encouraged me to take the opportunity to fix this water problem.

4. Is there an adequate budget to save it? With unexpected delays or problems, revisions to the plan or just wishful thinking, renovations always seem to cost more than the owner budgeted for. After thirty-three years in the business, David still finds budgeting one of the hardest parts of the job. Owners often forget to ask the contractor to price every part of the job—"Oh, you wanted that drywall painted, too?" Or the contractor lacks the experience to anticipate the complications a job will present. Have a solid plan, have the discipline to stick to it, and have a little extra cash set aside for what is called the balloon factor—count on 25 percent or so.

5. What's the impact on the environment? If you consider only what it takes to heat and cool a house, new construction is almost always more energy efficient: we just build houses more airtight than we used to. But a house that is already on-site has something called "embodied energy"—the resources that went into cutting the trees, hauling the lumber and other materials, and building the

house. One of my favorite upgrades to the house is my Bosch tankless water heaters, which deliver hot water on demand (key when you have lots of overnight guests), with ruthless fuel efficiency. Because I could seal the envelope of my home and modernize its heating and cooling systems, it made more ecological sense to save it. It's pretty routine for David Lee to get an Energy Star rating on new homes that he builds. It was cool to get one with an old home like mine.

David Lee and me conferring during the construction phase. David seems to be the one speaking here, a rare occurrence given how most of our meetings went. Quietly deliberate, David would hear me out as I talked through some piece of the design and, after asking a couple of questions, would find a way to make it happen. Our collaboration was proof that opposites are the best team.

< 2 >
REINVENTING THE HOME

I CLOSED ON THE HOUSE IN LATE FALL, THREE MONTHS OR SO
after I'd first seen it. That winter, my architect, Bob Eggleston, and I
walked through the house together on my visits to Skaneateles. Bob
was familiar with the house, having accompanied other clients who
were thinking of it as a tear-down. The family who built the place,
he said, had lived in Syracuse, and I later learned they had lived
around the corner from the house where I grew up. Their house in
the city was a big affair with plenty of bedrooms and a downstairs
centered around entertaining. Their lake house, which had stayed
in the family for decades, was a little escape by comparison. As close
as I could figure, it had two bedrooms up and two down, with a bath
on each floor.

PAGE 40: Looking through the media room toward the front door before transformation. PREVIOUS PAGES: David and I check on progress. ABOVE AND OPPOSITE: The previous owner's exuberant wallpaper in the downstairs bathroom incorporated figures of leaping deer. It inspired me to use a wildlife-themed covering on the ceiling when the bathroom became the powder room.

At some point, the house had been winterized—perhaps, we theorized, as a retreat for a family member who needed shelter during the Depression. It was updated, as a lot of American homes were, in the design booms of the 1950s and '70s. In these redos, the house must have shaken off a little of its camp-house look as the owners imported some of their in-town taste to the country. We found colorful and playful wallpapers (the powder-room paper featured stencils of deer romping in a forest). The light fixtures and even the closet hooks were distinctive— elegant here, whimsical there. The modifications had often been piecemeal, carried out by handymen like Howard, not part of a planned renovation. "Renovation by accident," Bob affectionately called it. Don't get me wrong: the

Picking Your Team: Architect

AS AN ARCHITECT WHO HAS SPENT HIS entire career in the Skaneateles area, Bob Eggleston had long known the family who owned the house, and about a year before I ran across it, he had had a chance to take a look inside. Strictly as a real-estate decision, he thought it was a toss-up—the house was not in bad enough shape to tear down, but not amazing enough, given the trend toward bigger and more glamorous houses on the lake in recent years, to convince any new owner to save it. Later, when Bob heard that an interior designer from New York, one who had his own television show, had bought the place, he was sure the house was a goner.

When we met, Bob was pleasantly surprised that I was planning to restore the house; I was pleasantly surprised to meet an architect who was so down-to-earth. As we talked, I realized that Bob met the most important criterion for any home owner looking for an architect: he was willing to collaborate on my vision. There are architects who drive around, I'm convinced, with a prefab Palladian-style window in their trunk, ready to tack it on the front of a house to brand it their own. Bob was ready to listen to my ideas and to turn my vision into construction plans.

Just as important, we shared a sensibility. Whenever I didn't have a strong concept of how a room or a detail should look, Bob always suggested something simple and clean. He was a natural partner for me.

As I got to know Bob better, I came to see his other great virtue as an architect: he knew nearly everybody in Skaneateles. A churchgoer and a dedicated volunteer in the community, he is a familiar face wherever he goes. He shows up at most town meetings whether he has something to present or not, and he appears frequently in front of the town's zoning and land-use committee. As they have watched the scale and ambition of houses on the lake explode, the powerful zoning board in Skaneateles has acted to protect the look and feel of the community and the lake itself. They have passed laws preventing construction too close to the shoreline or blocking others' views. They make you pay for every additional square foot of impermeable surface, and generally insist that waterfront home owners be responsible for what finds its way into the lake.

When it came time to get my changes through the committee, Bob knew how to present our plans as, he says, "a win-win" for both sides. When picking your architect, whether in a small town or a big city, for a zoning review or a co-op board, it makes sense to have someone on your side who knows the players and the institutional history of the community. An architect should be a guide who helps you play by the rules, look for mutually advantageous solutions, and keep your ego out of it.

ABOVE: Going over plans with architect Bob Eggleston (center) and Jimmy Splane, David Lee's everyday captain on the job. RIGHT: Alan Coffin was another indispensable member of David's team.

family had style. They just hadn't put the same kind of money into decorating their lake house as they likely had spent on their house in town.

The disparity was a reminder that what I was up to is a modern phenomenon. In 1917—or 1947 or 1967, for that matter—going out to the lake was supposed to be more like camping. You came out to get away from plush fabrics and complicated decoration; you were roughing it, even if you still had indoor plumbing and a kitchen stove. When these earlier generations of vacationers updated, do-it-yourself was part of the romance of a second home. "Renovation by accident" was just how things were done.

I wanted to preserve some of this simple approach. Americans, I think, are slowly real-izing that it's okay to have a humbler ethic about our homes—even our primary homes. After letting the building boom of the past few decades go to our heads, we are discovering that we don't need mudrooms as big as our parents' dining rooms, or kitchens the size of their living rooms. Modest but comfortable houses, which demand fewer resources, are more in step with our concern for the environment, which is driv-ing a "green" aesthetic of its own: there is a beauty in a structure that is in proportion to its use. Instead of size, the measure of a suc-cessful home is its ingenious use of materials, its reinterpretation of traditional forms, or its functional and clever layout. In architecture, character is becoming the new large.

My renovation was without a doubt going to be a modern update. I wanted a house that reflected the way I lived and entertained. Unlike a camp, with bracing deprivations like shared bathrooms and cots with wool blankets, my house would afford guests privacy and a little luxury: every bedroom would have its own bathroom, and all the furnishings would have a luxurious feel. At the same time I wanted to preserve the freedom and ease of a simpler time. I needed a retreat, not a complicated, high-maintenance showplace. I planned to achieve this by investing in the context and vocabulary of the house itself: practical solutions, natural materials, and details that were consistent with the original building.

OPPOSITE: As we dismantled the previous owners' hardscape, the layers told a fascinating history of American decor, one that had an impact on my choices. ABOVE: My design vocabulary of dark linen wall covering, tile in stony hues, and animal details was not so far off from the textured wall coverings and watery colors we had found in place.

The first summer after I bought the house was taken up with a lot of necessary improvements to the infrastructure. Besides beautiful new windows, I got a new septic system, new heating and cooling systems, and new insulation. I used the time to do architectural research around Skaneateles and make revisions to the design, but I also found plenty of ways to blow off steam.

The New Americana

WHEN I WAS IN SCHOOL, I ASSUMED Europe would always be the source of my inspiration. I traveled to Greece, Italy, England, and France and became conversant with the art in the Louvre. I'm not alone. American designers have long imitated the European aesthetic. Early American furniture is essentially stripped-down Queen Anne and Regency. Today we consciously copy European design with a sort of hip irony: Chippendale chairs painted a hot red, or a Louis-inspired dresser rendered in Lucite.

I love these ideas and have fun using them. As I spend more time in the industry, though, I have begun searching for a truly American point of view. The rest of the culture is already on this track. We no longer even depend on France, Italy, or Germany for a good bottle of wine—or even California. We drink wine from our own region, or we have a beer brewed down the road—or in the next room. We shop at the local farmers' market or wine store or supermarket to make sure we are eating and drinking fresh products. It isn't only a question of reducing our carbon cost; we're interested in the stories of American entrepreneurs and artisans who have turned a local resource into something amazing. We want our choices to bring us closer to the places we live in and love.

We should be able to think the same way when it comes to our houses. Classic Americana doesn't give us many choices. People buy up antique highboys and deck their walls with nineteenth-century portraits of people they aren't related to.

These styles are fine for a Yankee inn, but they are a testament to the idea that American design has stood still.

Redefining Americana was not on my agenda when I started coming back to Skaneateles. As I saw people all over central New York seeking to preserve their history in ways that worked for the moment we live in, I began to look at central New York, and the lake region in particular, as a case study in how American design might reinvigorate itself.

In the furniture I was designing I played with the fundamentals of traditional furniture, making them work for a twenty-first-century lifestyle. I would start with a midcentury-modern shape but cover it in a relaxed, textured linen to make it less precious. Then I'd add preppy piping and nail heads to give it a clubby, library feel. Add a brown waxed finish on the exposed wood arms and legs—a look you might see on an old dining table. Now you have a chair or a table that's not trying to be historical or modern, sophisticated or rustic—it's not trying to re-create anything. It's something authentic that also feels new.

I would subject my house to this same process. Starting with a structure made from stones from surrounding fields and wood from nearby barns, I could layer materials and details to give it a fresh start while honoring its past.

That doesn't mean I was interested in a strict period restoration. Scrupulously observing period can be a trap; instead of making design decisions, you become a museum curator. I wanted to return the house to the way its builder intended it—not for historical reasons, but to show that an old house, with a thoughtful renovation, can still live and breathe. What has changed is how we use our homes—how we entertain, what makes guests comfortable, how technology touches everything we do, how we mix casual with formal, classic with modern. I wanted a house that felt democratic and functional. This indelibly American structure over the years had lost its point of view. My job was to give it back its relevance—to take the fundamentals of its design, what was authentic and beautiful, and update them for a modern lifestyle.

If I accomplished what I was planning, the restored house would hardly give away what had happened. I wanted people to go by in their boat and say, "I never noticed that house before" or just "Wow, I love that house," not "Wow, did you see that new big house?" I wanted my friends to come see it and say, "I love it, but what exactly did you do to it?" I was reminded of the beautiful librarian who takes off her glasses and lets her hair out of the bun and suddenly she's a looker. It's the same woman. She's just revealing who she really was to begin with.

The question was, what kind of house had I bought? The design of the house was hard to classify precisely. Essentially the house was a mutt.

The most distinctive architectural legacy in central New York is the Greek Revival style. This part of the state first prospered in the 1820s and '30s, when Americans were con-

sumed with ideas taken from ancient Greek civilization. The fashionable homes of the time were modeled on the simple lines and rational proportions of classical Greek art and architecture. You can see these Greek Revival homes as you drive through towns such as Homer and Cortland. Squat triangular pediments sit atop columned porches with chunky moldings, either plain or with deep dentil details. Across the lake from my house, in the oldest part of town, there are a few beautifully updated homes from this era, and the banks and other commercial buildings in Skaneateles, built in the 1850s for what had become a bustling little city, are designed to look like miniature white Greek temples with their square, highly symmetrical facades.

By the time my house was built more than half a century later, Skaneateles had become a resort town. Wealthy families from all over New

ABOVE LEFT: A defining architectural look in central New York is the Greek Revival style that was popular when the region experienced a burst of growth in the mid-1800s. Skaneateles's prime example is Roosevelt Hall, with its soaring columns topped with a triangular pediment. **ABOVE RIGHT**: By the time my house was built in the nineteen-teens, the Shingle style had swept through, making its mark in particular on the house in the village known as The Boulders. **OPPOSITE**: With its multiple rooflines, some of which slope to within a few feet of the ground, my house has elements of Shingle style, among other influences.

The various architectural influences around Skaneateles, which include Italianate and Federal styles, allowed me to mix in lamps like this Federal style lantern that hangs next to the fireplace, below. Identical lanterns now appear below the peaked roofs with their Shingle style architectural brackets, above.

York refurbished the old Federal-style houses that had preceded the Greek Revival, adding Italianate details like carved foliage on the porch pillars. Just before the turn of the century, the Shingle style arrived, bringing more complex, rambling shapes and natural stone and shingle exteriors. (The Boulders is a prominent example of the Shingle style; it stands on the shore of the lake close to the village.) By the time my house was built, American architecture had entered a transitional period; it was a time of experimentation and flux. Homes with wraparound Victorian porches were going up next to Shingle-style mansions. Some home owners mixed architectural elements; others invested in replicating a particular style with a high degree of authenticity. My neighborhood in Syracuse, built around this time, became a design sampler: Spanish Colonials beside Tudors beside large Colonials.

Faced with all these competing influences, the people who built my house seem to have come up with their own combination. The exterior would probably be described as Colonial Revival, thanks to its symmetrical dormers on the lake side and its clapboard siding all around. Inside, too, despite cherry paneling and other rustic elements, the house took a lot from classic Colonial style—its rooms at the four corners of the house, for instance, symmetrically arranged around a central fireplace. But while a Colonial home is typically broken into discrete rooms connected by hallways, the rooms in my house flowed into one another without using hallways as transitions. This arrangement, which maximizes light and uses the available space most efficiently, is how we tend to design our homes today.

I saw other influences at work, too. From the road, the house appeared to have the low

sloping, irregular roof of the Shingle style. The use of timbers on the ceiling, while not the squared-off and crisply painted beams characteristic of the Shingle "cottages" of Long Island's Hamptons shore, also hearkened to that architecture's natural, rough-cut feeling, as did the craggy stone that made up the fireplace in my living room. And though the house was built long after the Greek Revival period had slipped away, there was something in the perfect symmetry of the nearly matched, nearly square rooms at either end of the house—the dining room and sunroom—that felt like a reference to Greek Revival structure. I would later draw on that motif in designing the dining room.

As I began to imagine the finished look of the house, I played with all these styles in my head—and more. Because the house was mostly a summerhouse, it would be natural to give it the breezy, cottage feeling of Nantucket and

The master bedroom with the three-quarter wall in place, punctured by the hole for the diamond window. The odd length of the room invited me to break it into two unequal parts to give me a conventional rectangle for a bedroom and a generous shower and sink area. Meanwhile, I accentuated the room's extensive length by running the V-groove wall paneling horizontally.

other seaside escapes. And given its location on a body of water that was once a major aquatic thoroughfare for its immediate area—and given my own love of boats—a few nautical references seemed well in keeping with the house.

These ideas all contributed to a vision that soon became a set of detailed drawings. Thanks to computers, I could involve my entire staff in the design of the house without any of us leaving Thom Filicia Inc. headquarters in Manhattan. To begin, Bob measured every room and exterior elevations and drew up plans of the house as it actually was. Then he e-mailed them to my office in SoHo, where my design team and I, as well as my partner, Greg, began to imagine a new life for the house. Everyone pitched in with their plans for the size, look, and use of every room. Inspiration boards, where we'd tack up photographs, drawings, and wallpaper and fabric samples, filled up over the course of a few

The finished master bedroom. Painted fresh white with black trim, the room has a classic nautical look. The horizontal paneling seems to imitate the boards of a boat hull. Balancing this seaside crispness is the punctuation of the rough wood barn post, which ties the room in to the natural materials used in the rest of the house.

weeks. The house was the topic of lunchtime discussions and after-work chats. Each time we thought we had a new version of the design, we compiled our changes to the floor plan on the computer screen and sent the file back to Bob, who then made his own suggestions. I spoke with Bob almost daily on the phone for several weeks that winter. Finally, Bob turned my office's CAD drawings into plans that could be put out for bids by contractors.

Ironically, working at a distance allowed me to see the house differently than if I'd only seen it up close, walking through with Bob in Skaneateles. Once I put the house's measurements into form, I could see the proportions of all the rooms. Looking at them all at once on the screen, I could see where I had space to tuck in a bathroom or add a closet, and how each room worked with the whole.

< 3 >
THE ESSENTIAL
ELEMENTS

THE PROVENANCE OF MY HOUSE WAS IMPORTANT TO ME BECAUSE it helped me to focus my decisions for the design process ahead. These days, the most frequently heard words in the design business are "editing" and "curating," but you rarely hear designers explain *how* they edit or curate. Many decisions are made by feel, of course—the result of the designer's education and the eye he or she develops over the years. I consider these things in my projects, but my work usually begins with the history and context of the property itself.

If the house has a distinct style—Tudor or Prairie Style—I'll follow its lead. When I've been asked to redecorate a Bing & Bing apartment on Manhattan's Upper East Side, I've brought the Bing brothers' characteristic Art Deco touches into the apartment itself. The association doesn't have to be explicit, however: sometimes I'll play off of an unusual architectural detail or something from the area's history. Without these references, the design feels artificial. A decor based purely on taste or passing trends ages quickly.

For my lake project, it was especially important to root the design in the materials. It was a big job that entailed hundreds of decisions and changes large and small. In renovating the structure, I had to know what to save, to preserve the spirit of the place. I looked for a short list of elements that defined it for me as a home.

In the end, I focused on three things to anchor my design: the five-plank wooden doors, the stone fireplace, and the paneled walls. All original, they captured what grabbed me about the house—its simplicity, its connection to its natural surroundings, and its American authenticity.

What this meant in practice was that any wood I added would build on the doors. All hard surfaces would look to the fireplace. The paneling would bind everything together. Whether I was trying to select colors, textures, or shapes, these elements would help me narrow my choices.

It may seem strange to want to limit choices, but it actually frees me to experiment. I can push boundaries or add counterpoint, secure that the design still feels organic to the house. I never lose my way.

The living room with walls and ceiling complete, just as the first pieces of furniture had begun to arrive. This room, the central gathering space in the house, contains on one wall (at left) all the defining elements of the décor—black five-plank doors, white V-groove paneled walls, and the rugged stone of the fireplace. Complemented by the rough-hewn ceiling beams, these elements would drive my choices for the design of the house as a whole.

THE DOORS

From the moment I saw them, I realized that the doors embodied the house's rustic charm. Dressing them up with a coat of black paint was exactly the transformation I envisioned for the entire house.

I'd never seen doors quite like the heavy wooden ones that stood sentry at nearly every doorway in the house: the person who built the house had most likely designed and made them. For that sense of connection alone, I liked them. They provided a link to the hand of the person who first made the place home. They also had an iconic presence all their own. I loved their imposing weight and hand-forged strap hinges. Where I could, I left the doors in their existing locations, and where they no longer fit because I'd expanded an opening or gotten rid of a wall, I moved them to another room.

No single element of the house ended up working as hard as the doors. They are a visual anchor in every room, communicating, through their heft and distinctive grooves, a rustic weight. I also needed them to establish a sense of formal sophistication. I chose to paint them

black, using a gloss from Pittsburgh Paints called Black Magic. All the paints in the house are low VOC (volatile organic compounds) and release fewer toxins into the air. These environmentally friendly paints aren't as glossy as regular paint, giving the doors a rich matte tone that I love. The paint sealed the wood—the finish, a worn-out cherry stain, had given up the ghost long ago—and transformed the doors.

I also upgraded the hardware. The existing handles were flimsy rim-lock-style pulls, like the kind you'd find on an old gate. They didn't match the crisp new black finish, nor did they properly latch. In a house where I expected a lot of guests, privacy was a necessity. I also needed locks that were dog-proof, so I could go to sleep and know that my two pups would not get out of my room before I woke, to bother my friends or be let out to roam by well-meaning guests.

The solution was to add a simple, black metal bolt lock. Easy to operate—who wants to fiddle with a foreign lock when you are a guest at someone else's house?—the bolt locks also function nicely as a door handle: installed just below eye level, they are perfectly placed to grab as you go in and out. And my dogs could neither reach nor move them.

This left me with the challenge of what to use as a doorknob below. I considered hand-forged lever handles that would match the hinges. I hadn't looked at many before I realized that period levers would look as if I was trying to be historically correct, turning my sophisticated black doors into something out of Colonial Williamsburg.

It wasn't until I was trolling through possible pulls for my kitchen drawers that I stumbled on the answer. The catalog showed various

ABOVE: Sun Valley Bronze is known for their chunky, handmade doors and cabinet hardware. After considering other handles that would have a historical look, I settled on these for the exterior doors, which had the right combination of rusticity and sophistication.
OPPOSITE: The satin nickel ring pulls for the interior doors granted the heavy black doors a touch of lightness and linked them to the nautical moments in the house.

sizes of satin nickel ring pulls. Bright metal pulls like these are used on boats as handles for lockers or hatch covers, usually mounted flush to the deck in a square of metal. The association with yacht hardware would introduce a nautical touch to my doors while also providing a bit of matte silver to complement their formal color. This fun, unexpected detail, meanwhile, would lighten the whole mood of the doors.

What had begun as rough wooden doors were now deeply layered, encompassing the formal and the rustic, nautical and camp style, historic and modern. They were also a template for all uses of wood in the house. I painted the kitchen cabinets—which my contractor, David Lee, made from three-quarter-

inch wood—with the same Black Magic color from Pittsburgh Paints, and I used smaller versions of the big doors' satin nickel ring pulls on the drawers. The wooden shelf above the kitchen shelf—a thick slab that evokes the doors' heavy planks—got the same paint color. The combination of black wood with a softly finished nickel has the same references to nautical detail, the same comfortable formality, the same counterintuitive blend of rustic and modern. By mimicking the look of the doors in the other woods in the house, I also perform a sort of sleight of hand, extending the old doors' feeling of age and authenticity to the parts that are brand-new. As a result my modern kitchen feels as comfortable in the house as the old doors—less like a renovation than a restoration.

The doors belong to another category besides "things made of wood." They also guard almost all the openings inside the house. Therefore they could serve as inspiration for every other kind of opening: the windows and exterior doors would also be replaced and their frames be painted formal black on the inside. Their crisp, finished look allowed me to dispense with window treatments where they would block the view.

The common color also dispenses with the need for consistency. The French doors along the lake side of the house are clearly more modern than the interior's wood doors—they evoke a turn-of-the-twentieth-century sophisti-

cation. Yet because they share the same color, their differences in period or style aren't jarring. The same consistency is applied to the kitchen cabinetry, the fireplace mantel—another slab of black wood—even the vanity in the downstairs guest bathroom, whose shape is neither rustic nor modern, but slightly Arts & Crafts in feeling. The common color, which ties all these woods and looks together, counteracts the lack of family resemblance.

In this way, each of my essential elements heads up a new list of things that go with it, from wall colors and tile choices to small details. When it came time to pick switch plates for the lights, I chose simple black plates, which read as old-fashioned but are surprisingly modern, just like the doors and the trim on the French windows. The black also distinguishes the technical sophistication of the lighting system, which is made by Lutron. At a time when lighting companies seem to vie to impress you with their complexity, this system is easy to operate and looks appropriate without being retro.

The decision practically made itself, and I could move on.

This shot of the upstairs guest room shows how the black gloss on the old doors allow them to play nicely with the finest materials in the house. Even cleaned up and restained, the doors could never have competed with the sleek gray wall covering shown here.

Country House, City House

YOUR PRIMARY RESIDENCE SHOULD feel like home. It needs to be highly functional, facilitating daily routines, from the quick escape to work and school in the morning to those catch-as-catch-can dinners when the busy members of the family reconvene briefly before going off to evening activities. Your second home should be an experience. It should force you to see things differently, slow you down and reflect its surroundings. Above all, it should be visually different. I always tell clients to make their breakfast table different from their dining table or an outdoor table—one should be round, one oval, one square. The differences will make for a unique experience in each place. The same applies to going from city to country. My New York apartment is very modern, with floor-to-ceiling glass walls. If my time in Skaneateles was going to be a relief from my city life, the decor had to be a change of pace as well.

THE FIREPLACE

Constructed from a pile of raw fieldstone, the five-foot-wide chimney rises from the massive hearth, dominating the living room's interior wall. The stack of earthy rock, the work of a guy named Bill Star, who built many fireplaces in the area, is a counterpoint to the shimmering water and ethereal light from the lake that constitutes the view in the opposite direction. The back of the fireplace makes up part of the wall in the media room behind it, and the chimney erupts, too, into the second-floor guest room, where it is again exposed like a river of rock climbing the wall. The fireplace's gray and brown stones, gathered from the surrounding fields as the house was being built, bring the landscape into the house in a very literal way.

As with the doors, I wanted to extend the fireplace's strong feeling of forest and field into other parts of the house. Where the doors influenced how I treated wood and the doorways throughout the house, the fireplace affected my decisions about countertops and tile. These hard surfaces are generally found in places where water flows—I wanted them to have the same graphic feeling of rock contained in the fireplace.

For my countertops, I turned to Vic Vallar, a second-generation stoneworker based in Syracuse but with contacts all over the globe. I told him I wanted a natural stone with lots

OPPOSITE: The fieldstones of the fireplace are the textural anchor of the house, not least because they make their appearance in the media room and upstairs guest bedroom as the chimney rises to the roof. With its visual weight and graphic natural surface, the fireplace inspired the other hard surfaces in the house.

of character, but muted—too high a polish or too strong a color, I felt, would bring too much of its own voice. Vic suggested soapstone, a relatively soft but very dense stone, composed mostly of talc, that repels the substances it's most likely to encounter in the kitchen—wine, vinegar, and oil. Soapstone needs more care than granite, but it has lovely veining and feels more organic and sleeker, especially in the subdued gray-black that complements the kitchen cabinets. Because my house is a weekend getaway, not my day-to-day place, I could afford to go with a higher-maintenance material for my countertops. The same soapstone serves as the sink surround in the powder room, where, along with black walls and bath fixtures, it provides a dramatic backdrop.

The tile I picked for the backsplashes in the kitchen and the bathrooms refers to the fireplace, too, though it is not made from stone. Drawing from Waterworks' collection of handmade tile, I employed a forest palette of mossy green and brown. The subtle differences in color, arising from the hand-applied glazes, give the impression of naturally occurring variation. I picked the unmatched browns of the octagonal tile I chose for the floor of the master bathroom's shower to evoke rocks in a streambed. None of the tile choices makes its points too literally. I avoided tile specifically made to resemble rock, or tile that had an unfinished, lumpy quality that shouts "handmade"—what my friend Barbara Sallick, cofounder of Waterworks, calls the "loving hands at home" style. The tile throughout the house is sophisticated but tight. From the fireplace to the shower, all the hard surfaces tell a single story.

The roughness of the chimney's stone practically demanded similarly tactile fabrics and wall coverings.

Tile

MANY PEOPLE, DAZZLED BY THE sheer variety of tile available, enthusiastically pick a different look for every opportunity. It's more important that the tile be tied to one idea, and therefore one material—even if you change the size and color slightly in each instance.

I turned to Waterworks because I knew the company commissions their own handmade tiles. Their crafted look would inject variation and personality into the narrow range of colors and shapes I had in mind. It didn't hurt that Waterworks, a small, American-owned company, operates in the same spirit of authentic, regionally focused design that was behind my Skaneateles house.

Authentic doesn't mean roughly finished or even rustic. Handmade tile—or Waterworks', anyway—has flat surfaces and square edges. At the same time, the human element means there are inconsistencies— for instance, in how much the glaze adheres along the edge of the tile—that present the eye with complexity and variation that mass-production techniques flatten out.

I picked three tiles in three sizes from Waterworks' Architectonics family of tile, all with a transparent glaze, which crackles for a nice finish and gives you a clean, pure look, because it doesn't obscure the tile's body. I combined the tile with a dark grout to emphasize the grid when the tile was applied to the wall, making for a stronger graphic look. (Using grout that's lighter than the surrounding tile tends to emphasize the surface of the tile.) If grout is not done properly, you lose the beauty of the tile.

ABOVE AND OPPOSITE: The understated stone colors of the tile create a calm, natural feeling in the downstairs guest bathroom (above) and in the master. At the same time, there is an elegance to the compact grid of the tile's arrangement on the wall. Kohler's uncomplicated, quasi-industrial fixtures finish the look.

V-GROOVE PANELED WALLS

Like the other elements I wanted to preserve, the paneled walls had been there since the house was built. This was not the plastic-looking brown sheets that say "suburban rec room," but thick, real wood planks of irregular widths with V-groove joining. Over the years, paneling has gone in and out of style, and as the family who owned the house redecorated, they had replaced much of the original wall with Sheetrock. I was determined to preserve what was left. However, as we began rewiring, upgrading the plumbing, and insulating the house to bring it up to code, and David Lee's team set about carefully detaching the paneling, most of it promptly crumbled. (The only original examples we were able to salvage stand on either side of the fireplace in the living room.)

Sheetrock would have been an easy option for the new walls. The renovation was turning out to be more extensive than I had anticipated; even with David faithfully saving what he could, the interior had become a gut job. Adding back the paneling seemed like a vain attempt to restore what was already gone.

At the same time, I didn't like my alternatives. Sheetrock leaves a room with no texture. Even with a liberal use of wall coverings—for which Sheetrock is the perfect underlayer—I

OPPOSITE: The virtue of using V-groove paneling throughout the house was to give it a common language that would mediate between all the stronger elements. ABOVE: The paneling had its own narrative, varying in color and surface, even imitating, as in the media room, the boldness of the doors.

would be left with walls I didn't love. Without the paneling, too, the house would lose much of its soul—the paneling was a key to the camp style. On that strong rustic base I could then layer different effects, as I did with the doors: white paint would contrast with the black trim to give the interior the crisp formality of a tuxedo, while recalling the relaxed, breezy air of waterside cottages. It would capture perfectly the combination of sophistication and casual cool I was looking for.

In the end we filled in with V-groove paneling on almost every wall. As I thought about each placement of new paneling, I took the opportunity to play—turning the paneling horizontal here, changing its color there, widening and narrowing the boards so that the walls pushed to the foreground or stepped back. Rather than let the consistency become boring, I used it to ground my design experiments.

It takes a trained eye to tell that the paneling is not as old as the rest of the house, when the eye focuses on it at all: the walls for the most part retreat and take a supporting role. But like any supporting player, the paneling performs a crucial role. It grounds all the other patterns and shapes going on in the decor, while making sure the colors pop against its placid white. The steady rhythm of its vertical grooves sets off the unruliness of the fireplace's rocky outcrop. It restores order beside the old, wonky bookshelves in the little hallway outside the powder room, for instance, where the house shows its age. In return, the bookshelves lend credence to the idea that the paneling is as old as they are.

BEYOND THE ESSENTIALS

The doors, paneling, and fireplace weren't the only parts of the house that needed saving. When I first saw it, the screened-in porch on the southwest side of the house looked like it was about to fall down. The owners at some point had enclosed the porch by erecting two facing walls—really a rickety jumble of screens, stained glass, and a sliding door—against a corner where the living room jutted out from the rest of the house. The interior walls of the porch were sided floor to ceiling in raw logs still covered in their bark. This was probably the original exterior of the house, and it made a great, graphic statement, a woody counterpart to the fireplace's unvarnished natural beauty. I decided to preserve the logs while making the porch a year-round room.

The timbers that stretch across the living room ceiling are structural, so I would have kept them even if I didn't consider them integral to the beauty of the house. Judging from the tool markings on them, they had mostly likely been cut and milled for a local barn fifty or so years before the house was built. Easily the oldest building materials in the house, they were a link to the area's past. So, in another way, were the stairs, though they were the newest part of the house. For whatever reason, the previous owner had put in a new staircase in 1964. I knew this

OPPOSITE: The sunroom's log walls were all the more powerful juxtaposed with tuxedo-crisp black walls and white trim. The next task was to furnish the space comfortably in patterns and textures that stood up to its extreme graphic quality without distracting from the walls—or your reading.

Reading the Context

WHAT IF YOUR HOUSE DOESN'T HAVE a clear style or defining details (or details that you like)? You create your own. Do a little research to find the prevailing style of the time that your house was built. Look for building plans or other archival material at the town hall or the local historical society. Even if your house was not designed with a readily identifiable style, the builder likely incorporated some general shapes or details from his or her time. Or with a little research you can judge your house's style yourself. Virginia and Lee McAlester's *A Field Guide to American Houses* is a good place to start your quest. The Internet also has a ton of sites that will help you get a sense of what the elements of a style are. As you gather information, you may see that your house shows signs of Modernism's clean lines, or Federal influence, or the simple forms of the Arts & Crafts' aesthetic.

If your house has a clearly stated style, you may want to expand on it. Put your house on a timeline of architectural fashions to see where its construction falls in the history of that style period. Sometimes, the design will show the influence of a style that came before or anticipated one that followed. You can look for opportunities to borrow a detail or two from these adjoining periods.

because the carpenter who made them signed his handiwork on a raw wood plank on their underside. (John Baker, wherever you are, come let me take your picture next to your stairs!) Open on one side, the stairs have a wonderful zigzagging sculptural quality, like an art installation that projects into the living room.

All these elements gave the house its character. They constituted the "good bones" on which the whole design would rest. The next step would be to clothe and accessorize them.

ABOVE: One of the longest-running discussions was the stair railing. The existing model was a nonstarter; it looked as if it belonged on a restaurant exterior. Its replacement, which appears on page 37, reminds me of a ship's rail. OPPOSITE: The stairs have a wonderful sculptural quality that I played up by painting them white to make them stand out from the oak flooring.

< 4 >

THE LIBRARIAN LETS DOWN HER HAIR

THE DESIGN OF A HOUSE ALWAYS OUTPACES WHAT'S HAPPENING ON the ground: You pick the tile, draw up the kitchen cabinets, and begin shopping for a washer and dryer before the demolition crew has finished dismantling the walls. You are working on curtains and cushions and bed linens while the electrician is still installing wiring. I'm used to this lag while the nuts and bolts of a project come together, but this time I was impatient. Every Wednesday, Alan e-mailed a new set of photos to update me on the team's progress and we found a reason to talk almost daily. But sitting in Manhattan all week made me feel like a dad who was missing seeing his children grow up. It wasn't just that it was my house—it was that, as winter turned to spring and David Lee and his men began to gently take the house apart, the story of the house continued to unfold.

One ongoing mystery was the dining room ceiling. It was a low affair with stained wooden beams—miniature versions of the living room's—dividing ordinary Sheetrock. Obviously a later addition, it nonetheless had enough character to suit me, without exactly wowing anyone. But from the house's perspective, the ceiling made no sense. It was lower than the ceiling in the screened-in porch, which had clearly been built to mirror the dining room in every other way. The disparity made us curious enough to knock a peephole through a wall while the crew was working upstairs to see what was above the dining room's ceiling. Looking crosswise, they saw only an unremarkable crawl space.

Some days later, however, Jimmy opened a small hole in the dining room ceiling in order to install a music speaker. Now pointing his light vertically, he noticed wooden planks that angled up toward the peak of the roof, with fir strips every six or so inches to accentuate their rise. I arrived that weekend to find a stepladder set up under a big hole in my dining room ceiling. Alan handed me a flashlight and invited me to take a look. I could see the original ceiling to the dining room. It rose another six feet, every bit as high as the sunroom's atrium ceiling, and was beautifully proportioned, like the roof of a tiny Greek temple.

Picking Your Team: Contractor

DAVID LEE LIVES IN AN OLD FARM-house dwarfed by its Victorian-era red barns. The oldest-looking building on his property is actually the newest: a one-story stone gem that looks like a modest church. David, it turns out, thinks even new things look better when they look old.

I'm not sure I was the ideal partner for David. I keep my watch set twenty-five minutes ahead of time in an attempt to correct my chronic lateness. David is extremely orderly. No matter how many projects he has going on, he seems to be on time everywhere he goes. I begin talking before I know what I mean and keep talking until I figure out what I'm trying to say. David speaks thoughtfully and briefly. As different as we are, I trusted him to do justice to the house because we shared the same goals. We wanted to preserve as much of the house as possible, then use quality materials to restore it to something that looked like it belonged on the lake. This is the most important criterion in picking a contractor: make sure you speak the same language. No matter how harebrained my ideas might have sounded to him at first, David trusted my vision and was willing to listen. As work on the house began, this mutual regard became crucial.

PAGE 86: Looking through the dining room from the kitchen. ABOVE: The framing of the dropped dining room ceiling is still in place as David and I discuss the atrium above it. BELOW: The atrium ceiling, wedded to the rest of the room by means of corner boards.

Not all my days in Skaneateles were that exciting. There was plenty of remedial work to be done on the basement, which was still filling up with water—runoff from the road at the top of my property—every time it rained. The septic system was being overhauled and enlarged while we converted the screened-in porch to a stable structure and into a sunroom, which meant digging out a basement below it so it could be connected to the heating and cooling system. David's crew spent days crawling into the hole and pulling the dirt out bucket by bucket. After a new floor was laid, we removed the logs on the outside facing wall in order to insert the doors to the deck and three new windows on the side wall to mirror the dining room's three, and to insulate the room.

I had little say in these necessary earthmoving operations, though they gave me time to bond with my next-door neighbor, Vinnie Byrne, who said that my new septic system was the most beautiful he'd ever seen. (His excitement may have been due to the fact that my old septic system had bordered his property.) The construction also gave me time to explore Skaneateles. Whenever I started to feel I was getting in the way at the house, I'd jump in the car or my boat and spend some time checking out other houses down on the lake or in town—to look again as a designer at a familiar place.

By this time summer was more than a notion. There were more people on the lake and around town, and more people coming up from New York City for a visit and to have a look at what was going on at the house. I was happy to give tours, happy to see the town again through my visitors' fresh eyes. I never came back without more ideas.

It was a time of constant thinking and improvisation, and constant questions. Every time my cell phone rang in Manhattan or wherever business had taken me, I expected it to be Alan or David or Bob calling, inquiring about some unanticipated opportunity or problem.

I was at my best when I was on-site, so I could walk through the solution in the house. Where did it make the most sense to put the light controls and the sound system? When the house was going full throttle in the summer, I thought, the dining room side of the living room would be the main axis of traffic, as guests arrived from the driveway or came downstairs and headed out to the deck or to the dock for a drink and a swim. The controls for the outdoor sound systems and a set of light switches for those activities belonged by the French door closest to the dining room. I located the controls for the indoor sound system not far from the front door, figuring that I would want to change the mood while greeting guests for a party or turn down the volume on my way to answer the door for a deliveryman or other visitor.

A typical summer day on Skaneateles Lake. Many residents have turned boathouses along the shore into guest apartments or entertaining spaces.

WINDOWS, INSIDE AND OUT

One of the things I studied most frequently on my outings was windows. I had two purposes in mind: first, to bring more light into the rooms that didn't face the lake, and second, to give these same walls, including interior walls, more visual interest. My plan was to place one window on the driveway side of the house into the powder room, one in the guest bath downstairs, and two more on internal walls between the master suite and its shower, and between the upstairs guest room and the stairwell. These would pull daylight through the house and add an interesting architectural element to the walls.

As with anything I added to the house, I wanted to make sure that what I was introducing was natural to the house and the area. My original idea was to use round windows, similar to the pair that had been placed on the garage, giving them a nautical look that was fully in keeping with the house; David had already ordered a set of five custom windows from the factory. In my trips around town, though, I saw no round windows. A few of the buildings in the Italianate style, built in the middle of the nineteenth century, had oval accent windows, but since my house had nothing to do with Italianate design, they weren't appropriate.

In town one day on an errand, I spotted a shape I'd never considered: a diamond. Elongated diamond windows sometimes appear on Queen Anne–style homes from the Victorian period, often as accents above a regular casement window. Shortly afterward, the Shingle style arose and architects sometimes borrowed the diamond-shape window frames to give their facades the deliberately informal, textured look they were after. I began to look for diamond windows in Skaneateles, and before long, I noticed more examples. Diamond windows would deepen the Shingle-style effect of the front of the house, I realized, while their strong diagonals would look modern and less romantic than an oval or round window. It was Bob who had the idea of turning square windows on their sides to make a modern diamond shape—and a less-expensive window. What's more, their pane dividers would naturally form an *X*—matching the *X*'s I'd placed on the ceilings.

Shortly afterward, the estimate for round windows came in. Together, the bill would have been about ten times what it would cost to turn square windows to get the diamond shape. The diamond windows were cheaper and they architecturally tied my house to the surrounding community.

Windows are a big-ticket item, and choosing them, therefore, always feels like a big decision. My existing six-over-six double-hung windows were terribly weathered by decades of northern winters and had to be replaced—but with what? With the striking diamond windows, the rest of the windows didn't have to be complicated—just something with enough detail to communicate what the house is about. I wanted wood inside so I could paint them, and aluminum cladding outside to withstand the weather.

All the better national companies sell windows that met my structural requirements, but a little-known brand called Eagle caught my eye as one that would best represent the spirit of the project. A small company based in Minnesota, Eagle had been acquired by Andersen in 2005 but retained the enthusiasm of a smaller brand still trying to build its name. When I called, their salespeople were excited to talk through my design with me. I also liked how their locks are integrated into the top of the window for a sleek modern look. This feature was important to me because I had decided on a window with a 1920s feeling, with two panes above and a single pane below, and I wanted them to trend a little modern. Eagle's windows fit the bill perfectly.

At night the windows become the star of the show. Guests gathering on the lawn and neighbors on passing boats will see the house as a set of windows.

FLOORS

The floors were a hodgepodge: 1950s brown interlocking tile in the front entrance butted up against three layers of carpet in the kitchen. All that would go without question. The living room presented a quandary. At some point a pegged oak floor had been laid over an existing floor. It was beautiful wood, with detail that fit the house nicely, but it was marooned a couple of inches higher than the adjacent floors, and as a result stuck out like a sore thumb. With the boldness of the fireplace and the doors establishing the rustic mood, the floors didn't need to make a similar statement. I encouraged one of the construction crew to disassemble the oak floor board by board and take it home, while I opted for a plain wood floor that would run through both levels, in a grain and color that receded quietly into the background.

I went to Lumber Liquidators to look at

their white oak flooring. For the simple effect I was seeking, their standard five-inch boards would be plenty fine. In fact, their A-quality wood was too fine, with long runs of relatively unblemished wood that would look out of place next to my raw rock and rough-hewn ceiling beams. For another thing, I didn't want the floor to be so delicate that I'd worry about walking into the house wet from a swim or cringe every time the dogs ran across it. On the other hand, Lumber Liquidators' C-quality boards, a utility grade with stubbier runs and lots of blemishes, were too rough. For what I wanted to accomplish, the B grade was just right: a variety of short and long boards with enough knots to give

OPPOSITE: The floors, the medium grade of white oak from Lumber Liquidators, came with plenty of character, which was emphasized with a white glaze.

Saving Is the Mother of Creativity

"BUDGET" IS NOT A BAD WORD IN any house project—economizing can actually force you to come up with solutions that are more creative and therefore more interesting than a high-priced choice. The brushed metal boat pulls on the doors are a good example—I could have spent hundreds more on handles that matched the French doors, but because I looked for something more affordable, what I came up with was not only more economical but cooler.

Another example was the sconces on either side of the fireplace. I needed a fixture that would not only hold up against the texture and weight of the stone fireplace but also connect to the rest of the house. I settled on the simple black outdoor lanterns from Restoration Hardware. These are a classic coach light, but the plain black metal box is modern without desperately trying to be so. And because outdoor lighting as a rule is less expensive than indoor fixtures, they helped me stay on budget.

OPPOSITE: Using a single flooring everywhere unifies the rooms, helping to pull together the wood finishes on the furniture and the window treatments.

it personality, but refined enough to serve as a proper canvas for my furniture.

Once the floors were down, we applied a glaze that would quiet them and at the same time give them a slight, sophisticated sheen. First we rubbed on an environmentally friendly, water-based white glaze with a rag, working in small sections of six-by-six feet. We would let the glaze sink in for a couple of minutes, then rag it off and move to the next section. The white glaze brings up the grain and the slight irregularities in the wood, which gives it a little bit of an etched look, approximating a Colonial-era method of protecting floors by sweeping ash from the fireplace into the grain. Using a commercial glaze is more immediate and easier and tones down the yellow highlights in the white oak floor.

After we let the glaze dry for several days, we mopped on natural tung oil in three coats, letting each coat dry for a couple of days. Tung oil is a good barrier against water or wine or whatever you might spill. Best of all, it isn't a polyurethane. Not only is it less toxic—especially for my dogs—but when the shine fades, or if you damage a small area, you don't have to redo the whole floor. You just repair and mop again with tung oil and let it dry.

Summer turned to fall again before the saws and hammers fell silent. David and I still spoke frequently, but I ran into him less often at the house. Eventually even Alan and Jimmy weren't there much. Our last protracted discussions were about the balustrade for the stairs. As usual, I described the different ideas I had

considered and why I had rejected them—a louver that would block the upstairs from view entirely (too dark), a series of metal squares with *X*'s inside them, to echo the ceiling (too Kentucky horse farm). When I explained what I had decided on—a simple structure of flat metal bars that evoked both a boat rail and a 1920s-style door grille—David nodded occasionally, asked a few questions, and left. Several days later, he called me back with a way to turn my sketches into a finished design.

I had spent nearly a year in the company of these artisans disguised as construction workers, discussing nearly every corner of the house, making big decisions and small ones alike. The house was in every sense a local product, thanks to Bob, David, Alan, Jimmy, and all the other talented people who put the puzzle together. The experience of working with them couldn't have felt more like coming home.

< 5 >
PUTTING IT ALL TOGETHER

MY FIRST CONSIDERATION IN DECORATING A HOUSE IS NOT HOW it is going to look, but how it will be used. A dining room that will see lots of dinner parties requires ample seating, plus a shot of quiet glamour. A room intended for lounging with the Sunday paper calls for furniture that you can put your feet on. We eat everywhere, so it only makes sense that our living room coffee tables be able to accommodate glasses and plates, and that impromptu seating be available nearby. Decor, in short, should be fact based. It should be a reflection of how we live.

How we live—how we spend our free time, how we dress, how we entertain—is less formal nowadays than at any time in our cultural memory. The modern lifestyle is unpretentious, casual, spontaneous.

Yet we are devoted to design. We love fine things and make them part of our everyday routines. The signature outfit of our era is a Chanel jacket and jeans. We love to combine textures, colors, and references from every period and culture.

The art of decorating in this environment comes down to balance—successfully mixing the refined and the relaxed. In a vacation house like mine, the atmosphere skewed toward the casual—my guests would spend a lot of days tromping in and out in bathing suits, and even dinner parties are often spur-of-the-moment, giving nobody time to get home to dress. A decor that caused someone in a T-shirt and jeans to feel out of place wouldn't do. At the same time, the interiors should make guests feel special, and while I would never host a stuffy formal dinner at the house, I liked the idea of spending holidays there. But for that to work, the house would need to dress up as well as dress down.

We find this mix of casual and sophisticated by balancing the vocabulary of design. The dialogue among texture, color, material, and finish operates at an almost subliminal level, pleasing the eye without the beholder noticing. It deepens the entire experience of each room.

The hardscape already granted me a wide range of surfaces: the corrugated look of the doors and the paneling, the raw timber and stone, brushed metal, matte finishes, and dark tile. Overall, though, the effect of these strong elements was pretty stark, leaving me plenty of room to balance them with plush fabric, polished metal, and painted and stained wood.

Balancing the different components of a room is a bit of an art, and like any art the goal is to get the effect without calling attention to what you're doing. Some juxtapositions can declare themselves broadly, of course; in the living room I purposely placed chrome end tables at either side of the Skaneateles sofa and topped them with polished nickel lamps. With all the dark wood on the sofa, I wanted to add some zing; the lamps' bright modernity gives that side of the room a nice kick in the pants. But when it came time to add a few chairs around the room, I was careful to introduce the different notes incrementally: each new chair I added has exposed wood legs or arms, but here the wood is finished in a traditional walnut stain, there it appears almost black, for a more modern feel. The shift in tone is never jarring because each piece changes one thing while carrying forward something of the others. The room always remains coordinated and balanced.

Balance doesn't have to be restricted to any expected list of features—color or texture or finish. Every piece of furniture has a hundred attributes for which you can find opposites to create an aesthetic tension. Chairs can be vintage or contemporary, delicate or solid, classic or truly American; patterns are abstract, organic, or geometric. Any of these aspects can be used to contrast pieces or link them together. Or you can be completely subjective. The curtain fabric in the sunroom has a random abstract pattern that distinguishes itself from the solids and geometrics in the room, but it goes with the intense natural feeling of the raw log walls because the pattern reminded me of raindrops.

OPPOSITE: The rough rope lamp base echoes the natural feeling of the home. Its curvy form adds a note of playfulness in the guest bedroom.
ABOVE: A wire sculpture of an anchor supports the nautical feel of the boathouse.

PLAN, THEN CHANGE YOUR MIND

To be certain a room makes sense, you need an anchor: the progression from piece to piece has to begin somewhere. For the living room the starting point was the Skaneateles sofa; for the dining room the decor sprang from an idea of a classical Greek pavilion. I often liken decorating a house to shopping for a meal. You start with one thing you know you are going to make—your entrée. Then you think, What do I want for a side dish? Or, How can I add a little color? How can I add something unexpected? What flavors go with that?

Then you go shopping, keeping an open mind and letting your eye roam. Random finds are a good and necessary phase of the work.

If you scrupulously plan what you're going to cook, you can run through the supermarket quickly, grabbing the precise ingredients that you need from the list you brought with you. But if you stick too relentlessly to your shopping list you won't be able to take advantage of vegetables in season or a great deal on something you hadn't thought of. If you spend hours planning every moment of the meal, your guests will taste it; the whole evening will feel stale before it starts. Be ready to adapt your

Make room for spontaneity whether it's a joke like a cigarette in a mounted deer's mouth (see page 160 for the full story) or a last-minute switch in the living room rug.

plans to include what's in season or what's on sale at the grocery store.

By the same token, I always keep an open mind when working through the final details. As furniture began to arrive in summer of 2010—from my place on Copake Lake, from my furniture company, from my office—I gave myself room to incorporate surprises. A beautiful pair of rattan chairs appeared from Missy, the mom of my old friend Brooke. When rugs from my collection with Safavieh arrived, I changed my mind about where I wanted them to go. When I saw the rug intended for the upstairs guest room—a blue background with a white cascading pattern inspired by the image of rushing water—in the living room, a few feet from where the delivery guy put it down, I realized that the pattern brought a note of deep color to the room, giving the downstairs more gravity. The connection between the water theme of the rug and the lake view out the living room windows also made it feel right.

I'd been debating between an ottoman and the low table I'd specified for the sunroom. At the last minute I swapped it for a Bish Bash bench instead. Its simplicity counters the staidness of the chairs, and it goes nicely with the sofa in that room. Most of all, it breaks up the feeling that everything's perfect; as a result, the room breathes.

There's a difference, in other words, between coordinating a room and smothering it in decisions. You should have the foundation of the room established, but you don't have to organize everything to the point of being painful. Make bold moves where you are inspired to, decide on the pieces you really want, and then support them. When I ended a wall with a weathered barn post in my master bedroom, I chose curtain fabric with a similar brown color and with a leafy pattern that would refer to its wood grain. Now the post isn't standing alone.

When rooms are put together in this way, the people who occupy them register the attention to detail, even if they can't put their finger on what makes the space feel good.

Introducing a bit of humor is the easiest but most overlooked part of decorating. For instance, a formal portrait of my dog Paco in the living room (opposite) gives guests permission to relax and have fun.

ENTRANCE HALL
WHITE PANELED WALLS · BLACK DOOR · STABLE HOOKS · BLACK METAL CEILING LIGHTS · JAMESVILLE BENCH · MIRRORED CANDLE SCONCES

OPPOSITE: The entrance hall, even at its expanded size, is small, but guests get an immediate promise of the lake views. As I take their coats and get them a drink from the nearby bar, their anticipation of the treat they have in store builds.

I loved this space from the moment I came into the house. Admittedly, it was unlike any entry hall you'd build in a home today. Instead of the vaulting atriums that have become commonplace, the small foyer that greeted you inside the front door of my Skaneateles house was the size of a decent Manhattan closet. The front door barely cleared the wall opposite and the ceiling, which is low to accommodate the stair landing directly above it, so it feels like it is sitting on your head. I did add a dozen or so square feet of floor space by bumping out the front wall three feet. I could have reoriented the stairs to open up the entire front of the house, but in the end, I kept the room small and the ceiling low. Entering under the staircase felt

old-school, and it establishes the age of the house as soon as you come in.

In the same way, from the time a visitor approaches the front door—custom built, based on the heavy plank doors inside—the basic elements of the design found in the rest of the house emerge: paneled walls in white, with a black light fixture that's rustic in its materials but with a spare modern look.

The furnishings are about function—this room is about getting you settled. The Jamesville bench provides a place to put down packages while you get your wrap hung up on the stable hooks, or to sit and untie boots, which can be stashed underneath. An umbrella stand in the corner completes the sense of the utility of the space. The plain lines and handles of the bench and oversized barn hardware add to the historic feel.

Rather than wow guests, the entrance hall is the setup for a big reveal—something I had learned from doing television. Not until a guest has been greeted and looks down the hallway past the stairs does he or she spot the lake and begin to appreciate the many dimensions of the house.

OPPOSITE: The entrance hall's oversized coat hooks and St. James bench make this small space a friendly, casual introduction to the house, as does the usual collection of shucked-off shoes. By the time guests have put down their things, they are already feeling relaxed.

A niche in the wall became a natural place for
a series of prints; the rope rail on the stairs
introduces the nautical element in a gutsy way.

KITCHEN

SOAPSTONE COUNTERTOPS • PAINTED WOOD CABINETS •
NICKEL-PLATED CHICKEN-WIRE CABINET PANELS • STAINLESS
STEEL APPLIANCES • STAINLESS STEEL–TOPPED TABLE
WITH WORK STOOLS • CHROME AND WOOD ÉTAGÈRE •
BULKHEAD LIGHTS

OPPOSITE: On weekend days, the kitchen's
stainless-steel-topped table is headquarters—
a place to go through mail, read the paper, or
plan the day over coffee. When we're entertaining, the table acts as a divider between
the chef's sink, fridge, and stove and the area
where guests are greeted.

For Greg and me, the kitchen is our first stop upon arriving home. We shuttle in from the entry hall to put down what we've brought in, turn off the alarm, get a quick meal started, or fix a drink after a long drive from Manhattan. It's an office, too, where we get the day's phone messages and go through the invitations and letters that we've just pulled out of the mailbox. It's a place to stop in for a quick bite, or a sanctum where one of us (usually Greg) can whip up a meal for ten while communicating easily with the guests.

In other words, like many American kitchens, ours is designed to allow us to do a lot of things at once. My task was to create distinct areas for all these demands in a space that was not only relatively small but narrow—I didn't want the kitchen to feel like a hallway.

The area nearest the front door is all business. A sturdy stainless steel table is there to receive groceries, packages, and keys, and to provide a surface to write on. When I come up from meeting the mail boat in the summer months, I sort letters there as I drink a cup of coffee. On the opposite wall are deceptively deep and tall cabinets with ceiling-high slide-out shelves hiding a pantry for stowing groceries. A five-shelf étagère to the right accommodates

overflow boxes of pasta or other delectables, as well as items that are both handy and attractive when cooking or entertaining—candlesticks, mixing bowls, and vases for flowers.

Where the side door to the house once was is a bar, complete with a wine fridge and work sink. With a deep countertop below a set of glass shelves, the bartender (usually me) has everything at hand. To the right is a space for glassware and a Viking ice machine, the best I've ever owned. Below is a liquor cabinet and wine fridge (Viking again). When we're having people over, the bar becomes my station where I can greet guests, get their drink orders, take flowers they've thoughtfully brought and pop them in a vase from the étagère—all without running myself ragged dashing from door to kitchen or getting in the way of the cook.

This part of the kitchen's social function is reflected in the design. The white cabinets carry through the wall color from the entry hall, signaling their common purpose as places where guests are welcome. The transition from entry hall to kitchen is hardly noticeable as they come in with bottles of wine or dessert.

The decor changes drastically in the chef's domain. Dark colors and metal surfaces don't

Beyond the kitchen sink is the neighbors' fence, so I brought the windows down low, where they provide light to work by, and put shelving at eye level and above. The shelves store bowls and other necessary and attractive pieces. **FOLLOWING PAGES**: The cooking area, with its professional stove and open cabinets fronted in nickel chicken wire, is partly rustic, partly sophisticated, and all business.

just hide spills and make for easy cleanup, they broadcast that something more serious is going on in this part of the kitchen. Bulkhead lights on either side of the sink build on the idea of this area as a workspace—if a refined and elegant one. (They also build on the nautical theme of the ring pulls and boat-cleat cabinet handles.)

It was important to have a great environment for cooking. Though we use the house only on weekends and holidays, entertaining is at the heart of what we do here, and I didn't want to stint on the equipment. The Viking appliances give it a professional look and feel, and the company fits the classic American viewpoint of the house. It's the same reason I used Kohler faucets and sinks throughout the house, products that, in their design and fabrication, read American and give me a wide range of styles. They present one aesthetic without being redundant or boring.

The transition between the two halves of the kitchen is the stainless-steel-topped island. I fooled around for months with designs for a custom built-in peninsula cabinet that would do this job, but in the meantime stumbled on this table with heavy square teak legs and red stools. It complements the mood of the house, and its top is rugged enough to handle the wear and tear of cell phones, key chains, flower-arranging tools, coffee cups, and mixing bowls. It also has a low shelf for storing bowls and baskets.

OPPOSITE: A paper figure of a ram's head covers a wall sconce that, when lit, gives off a gentle glow.

OPPOSITE: The bar, surrounded by floor-to-ceiling storage and a Viking wine fridge, allows me to greet guests with a cocktail of their choice. ABOVE AND RIGHT: Just inside the kitchen near the entry is a handy étagère and the phone, accompanied by the house's Energy Star plaque.

The table has a presence in its own right—it's a place for casual breakfasts or an afternoon cup of coffee with a magazine. For the cook, this adaptable piece of furniture is highly strategic. He can annex the table's stainless top when counter space has run short elsewhere; more important, it's a barrier to keep guests (and bartenders) out of his path. The table protects the kitchen's tight but perfectly comfortable triangle from sink to stove to refrigerator. Overhead I hung a papier-mâché ram's head that I had in my Copake house. It's one of my favorite pieces because it lends some whimsy and a sense of ambience to the room, and here it seemed to go with the deer heads. The ram covers a wall sconce that lights it from within, lending a little mood lighting. The unusual piece also offers a conversation starter for arriving guests.

The transformation isn't total: uniting the kitchen is the single style of pulls for the drawers, and the backsplash behind the stove and over the bar sink are tied together by their similar tile. But the vocabulary of the cooking area is quite distinct. The upper cabinets were inspired by the cold cellar (often called a French pantry) that the previous owners had built in the basement. I imitated their chicken-wire doors, but in a silver nickel finish that lends them a kind of country-chic.

When I removed the swinging butler's door that separated the kitchen from the dining room, I replaced it with a wide, square arch to keep an easy communication between the kitchen and the dining room, so guests don't feel too much pressure to entertain themselves. But I was also conscious that the kitchen, though it was just the size we needed, is relatively small by today's standards. A key to working happily in a space like this is to keep the sight lines open—to the lake for a sense of greater space and to the dining room so the host can cook and interact with guests.

Because the cook's side of the kitchen is so open to the dining room, I wanted to smooth the transition here, as I did between the bar area and the entry hall. There is an architectural feel to this part of the kitchen, and a symmetry that prepares the eye for the dining room's formal rigor.

The kitchen viewed from the dining room table. The cook has enough privacy at the stove, on the right inside the kitchen doorway, to get the job done, but can easily chat with guests.

DINING ROOM

BLUE LINEN WALL COVERING • FISH-EYE NAIL-HEAD DETAIL • ATRIUM CEILING • WHITE CORNER BOARDS AND BASEBOARDS • BLACK WINDOW AND DOOR TRIM • GREEK KEY CURTAINS • BURLAP DOME PENDANT LIGHT • BORODINO DINING TABLE • GREEK PEAK CHAIRS

The dining room was destined to be a warm, intimate space, not a grand dining hall; this house is about getting away and getting together. After a day of running around town and to the club and going out in the boat, I want my guests to be reunited in an atmosphere that's contained and cozy.

When I first saw the room, it was ringed in wainscoting that rose only as high as your knee. This treatment—probably done that way to accommodate the low ceiling—made the room look like it belonged in a dollhouse. When we took out the low ceiling to reveal the original atrium peak, we took out the wainscoting, leaving no trim except the door frames. This had the odd effect of making the ceiling look disconnected, like a hat floating above the room with nothing holding it up. To correct this, I had David insert corner boards to connect the baseboards to the ceiling. On the walls between them I put blue linen wall covering, which makes the corner boards stand out like lithe white columns, increasing the impression of sitting in a tiny Greek temple.

I accentuated that classical Greek look by using my klismos-inspired chairs around the dining table and by making the curtains from a natural cotton fabric—like all the fabrics in the

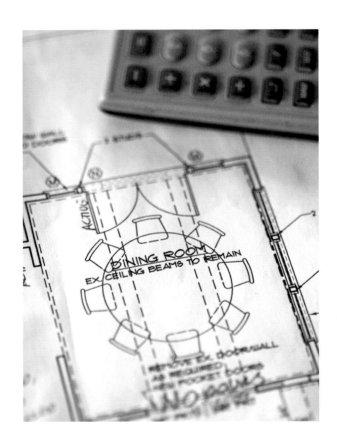

OPPOSITE: The dining room, ready for an informal lunch on a summer day.

house, it's from my line with Kravet—stitched with a slightly abstracted Greek key motif. I normally trim my curtains with a cuff that matches the height of the baseboard, and here I used the same blue linen that is on the walls. To accentuate the height of the ceiling, I brought the curtains to the highest point I could.

By day, the room is fresh, smart, and crisp, thanks to the white trim outlining the blue linen. When the French doors are open, the freshness of the room increases the feeling that we're sitting outside. By night, the height of the ceiling creates a sound-deadening volume of dark space above the diners' heads. The deep blue linen recedes into the darkness, pulling everyone together.

To increase this effect, I kept the room very sparsely furnished to reduce the surfaces that might pick up reflections from the chandelier's circle of light. My large round Borodino table, which satisfies my wish for a place to host ten people for dinner with a minimum of fuss, takes up most of the available space anyway. There's no sideboard, and on the walls only black iron candle sconces. The loose weave of the linen soaks up the noise of silverware on dishes and even softens the diners' voices.

To give the room an air of celebration and sparkle, around the trim I added fish-eye nail heads with a finish that looks almost tarnished. They are quieter than conventional nail heads, but against the blue walls they have a jewel-like elegance. Even in the darkness at the edge of the room, their patina glints softly.

Everything else in the room works to soften the rather tailored, coordinated look of

Treating the Windows

In Skaneateles I avoided curtains where I wasn't worried about sun fading the furniture, but in the dining room they were part of the tailored look I was interested in. As I often do, I gave my Greek key curtains a contrasting cuff at the bottom, matching their height to that of the baseboard so that everything lines up nicely and the curtains are integrated into the architecture of the room.

On the side window, I needed some kind of treatment for texture and warmth, but I didn't want a heavy curtain. Instead, I used a Conrad shade made of a beautiful handwoven silklike blue yarn created from arrowroot and palm fiber. It has an unusual weave that makes it drape in the middle, and it filters light beautifully. I chose it as my default shade in the house. Using the same shade throughout the house gives the windows a consistent look from outside.

the fabrics. The finials on the black metal curtain pole are in a bleached finish that picks up the slightly distressed look of the Geneva gray table. The lighting fixture I chose, Restoration Hardware's burlap dome pendant, was designed with Morrocan style in mind, but in the context of the house, it reads like a rustic, utilitarian fabric. The various chairs in the room, none of them matching the table exactly, also contribute a more idiosyncratic, collected feel.

To give the dining room a tailored look, I used the same blue linen on the walls to cover the seats of my Greek Peak chairs, and reprised the walls' nail head details. With just two colors and elemental accessories in the form of iron candleholders, the room is layered without being stuffy.

LIVING ROOM

WOVEN WALL COVERING • WALL BANDS • OUTDOOR LANTERNS •
PANELED CEILING • WEEDSPORT CHAIRS • SKANEATELES
SOFA • NIAGARA RUG • STRATHMORE CONSOLES • BRATTEL
ROAD ARMLESS CHAIRS • WENDELL TERRACE COCKTAIL
TABLE • FRENCH FORT BENCH • DRUMLINS LAMP TABLES

OPPOSITE: Open to the lake, the living room changes mood with the sky and water outside. Its variation of texture, color, and finish allows the room to respond to different qualities of light and weather.

The long living room is the crossroads of the house, where guests first see its full scope, or pass through on their way to the lake, or rally before an outing. It is also the salon—somewhere everyone can lounge, eat, warm themselves at the fireplace, or socialize while watching the parade of boats go by on the water. Unlike the modern "great rooms" that have become the center of family life over the last couple of decades, my living room is a little old-fashioned. Great rooms divide the space into distinct eating, gaming, and TV-watching areas, whereas my living room invites guests to

the center. They naturally break up into conversational groups, but the formal structure of the room, focused on the Skaneateles sofa with the view of the lake behind it, holds the larger group together. Chairs and stools radiate out from the sofa, so more chairs can be pulled in from the fringes as the party grows. Seating can even be grabbed from adjacent rooms.

The furniture is a kind of conversation as well. The Skaneateles sofa combines a midcentury-modern shape with traditional detail, so on either end of it I placed an armless chair upholstered in pale brown leather with legs painted black. The sexy shape of these low chairs pushes the room toward the modern.

To introduce a third thought to mediate between the modern and traditional finishes, I chose my chunky Wendell Terrace oak coffee table finished in bleached-out Geneva gray and winded oak consoles. Those finishes account for all the wood dispersed strategically through the room. The walnut appears on the Weedsport chairs and in the French Fort bench. The gray finish appears on the side chairs, on the consoles that stand at either end of the room, and in a subtle echo, on the window's finials. The Geneva gray also connects the living room with the dining room and its Geneva gray table.

Meanwhile, the metal tables and mercury glass lamps at either end of the sofa are supported, too. The polished chrome hurricane

Matching chairs, tables, and lamps placed symmetrically echo the structure of the house itself, while relaxed fabrics and rugged surfaces balance the visual formality with a sense of approachable comfort.

lanterns on the console pick up the silvery tables and lamps by the sofa, reinforced by the handles on the back of the Brattel Road chairs, the struts on the French Fort bench—even the chrome cleat that secures the mirror on the mantel. Nothing is random; there is a common thread that runs through it all, but no strictly regimented hierarchy of materials, accents, and finishes. Instead there is a rhythm to how each is presented and then echoed across the room.

The living room leans more toward the modern than any other room in the house, including its palette. Pale beiges and grays combine with pops of strong red and blue. The large pictures at either end of the room, from a

OPPOSITE: The wall covering I chose to work with the wood is a favorite of mine, a Phillip Jeffries linen that I've put in several clients' projects. Each time I do, I think how I'd like to live with this someday. ABOVE: Foxy relaxes on the Skaneateles sofa.

collection I created called Memories, play with nostalgia, but the photographs are purposely blurred, lending a modernizing distance to the familiar beach scenes. They are familiar without being overtly personal. The unbroken, easy, flowing space emphasizes this modern airiness.

Counteracting this contemporary openness are the big statements of the fireplace and the beams overhead. They kept my design from straying too far from the spirit of the house. I reinforced their imposing look with the iron-black ring around the mirror on the mantel, paired with the outdoor carriage lights from Restoration Hardware on either side of the fireplace, but I wanted to keep the room from feeling too heavy. In the curtains I echoed the natural wood and stone with the rug's watery pattern and the orange-red stitched leaf shapes in the curtains.

For a wall covering, I chose one that I've put in several clients' projects, a Phillip Jeffries Amalfi Silk linen. When I used it in a client's Manhattan loft, I immediately knew I'd like to live with it someday. Composed of woven paper over a matte black background, it has a wonky imperfection that makes it compelling—people always want to touch it. Its black background locks in the black of the double doors, and even refers to the fish-eye nail heads in the dining room. But what I like best is its ethereal lightness and visual calm.

To pull the walls together, I added horizontal bands of white painted wood. This inexpensive detail produces a refined architectural effect with strong structural lines that turn the rest of the wall to background. If you took the covered surfaces of the walls away, it would seem as if the ceiling were still standing.

What I am happiest about is the way the living room works. When we entertain a big group, the food goes on the console near the kitchen. The second console is set up as a bar. We can seat plus-or-minus a dozen people around the living room—fewer if they are eating, more if they are sitting for drinks and something to nosh. I know a party is a success when I spot two people sharing one of the armless chairs, sitting more back-to-back than side by side, one talking with the group on the sofa, the other to someone by the fire.

OPPOSITE: Amid all the natural stone and water hues in the room, I used artwork to inject a modern punch of bright color. FOLLOWING PAGES: Abstracted architectural references counter the modern with a feeling of weight and history.

inside cuba

PHOTOS BY GIANNI BASSO / VEGA MG
TEXT BY JULIO CÉSAR PÉREZ HERNÁNDEZ
ED. ANGELIKA TASCHEN

TASCHEN

THE MUSEUM

Passion for Progress

Solid shapes of stone and wood and classic
references anchor the living room's furnishings
in the landscape and the house.

Each finish in the living room is repeated from the center of the room to its corners. The detail on the back of the Brattel Road chair echoes the metal lamps on the sofa's end tables; the arm of the Weedsport chair and the curtain hardware are part of the tight regime of wood finishes.

SUNROOM

RAW LOGS • BLACK PANELING • CAZENOVIA SOFA • CENTURY CLUB CHAIRS • SOLVAY SPOT TABLE • BISH BASH BENCH • ANCHOR ROPE CHANDELIER • DEER TROPHY

The sunroom stands opposite the dining room, and the two rooms are opposites in other senses as well: one is squarely in the active traffic pattern, the other is a cul-de-sac. The dining room is about entertaining groups; the sunroom is a comfortable space that invites you to get cozy, to settle down to read, sit for a long telephone call, enjoy a quiet conversation with a couple of companions, or simply gaze at the lake. It is a perfect contrast to the dining room, with its refined design references and crisp color scheme. The two rooms—one untamed and rustic, the other tailored and classical—represent the extremes of my design.

The sunroom's full impact only becomes clear when someone crosses the living room and enters it. Only then do the logs that cover the vaulted ceiling and interior walls come into view. The raw, wildly graphic logs are always unexpected and prompt a gasp. In fact I toned the sunroom down from its original condition, replacing some of the logs with paneling. Ironically, adding the more sedate paneled walls celebrated the rough logs more. The paneling frames the logs so that their randomness can be appreciated, and they look even odder next to a finished wall, which I painted a calming black for good measure. Last but not least, because the two walls that are visible to visitors approaching from the living room are paneled,

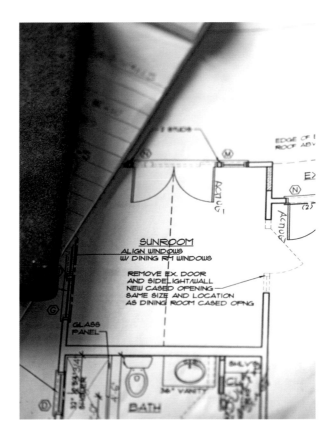

OPPOSITE: I had no intention of taming the unvarnished bark of the log walls in the sunroom. Instead, I set them off with the contrasting, formal black walls and white trim. Then I complemented their graphic natural weight with the chunky shapes of the club chairs, tufted leather on the Bish Bash bench, and raw hemp in the chandelier. The result is a room of extravagant comfort and a surprisingly contemplative mood.

The rope chandelier and the refined but tactile hand of the chambray establish the range of surfaces in the room. The chandelier brings in a hint of nautical flavor.

the surprise of the unruly logs is preserved for as long as possible.

The roughness of the tree bark demanded that I meet it with a variety of deep textures: wool felt, leather, linen, mohair. These were precisely the feel I wanted in what I envisioned as a masculine retreat, recalling a lounge in a men's club. The Century Club chairs, covered in a textured wool-and-linen fabric in a gutsy, nubby chevron—my version of herringbone—with a line of piping along the cushions' seams, captures this aesthetic nicely. The sofa, with its high back, is covered in a woolen felt close to limousine cloth, and the seat is of velvet mohair. The rug on the floor is thick wool. A chandelier made of rope and hemp twine holds its own

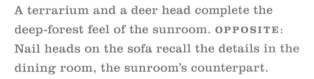

A terrarium and a deer head complete the deep-forest feel of the sunroom. OPPOSITE: Nail heads on the sofa recall the details in the dining room, the sunroom's counterpart.

against the ceiling and brings in a nautical note and more rough texture. Even the articulated chrome reading lights, added to reflect some light and give the room a touch of modern zip, have the feel of a gentleman's retreat.

The black walls complete the masculine tone of the room. Nowhere else in the house does the color seem as complex as it does here, where it is drenched in light from the French doors, and it is played against the grays, browns, and greens of the outdoors and the bark on the walls. As complex as this space is, it retains the soul of the screened-in porch it replaced.

A deer head, given to us as a housewarming present by our friends Mark and Megan, was perfectly at home in this room and led to a number of deer-oriented gifts—some genuine trophies like this one, skulls from small animals, and sculpted trophy heads and antlers from vintage stores. Since I'm not a hunter, people who know me are surprised to see this guy in here. But its very unexpectedness adds humor to a room that is pretty buttoned-down. An unknown party guest lightened the effect of one deer head by sticking a half-smoked cigarette into its mouth. Now when people ask me if I shot the deer, I tell them that he died from smoking.

The contrast of the forest elements—including a fern planted directly in the logs—and the lake views (opposite) make the sunroom a perfect expression of the surrounding landscape.

Using Color

I USE QUITE A BIT OF COLOR, BUT I neutralize its effect. If I told you I was going to take a red chambray sofa, pair it with a green ottoman, and put yellow cushions on it, you'd blanch. Now look at the sunroom: that's precisely what I've done. The red is earthy, the green a pale hue found in nature, the yellow a quiet mustard. Muting the colors in this way allows you to feel the color without having it overwhelm the room. The upstairs guest bedroom is all about blue, yet none of my guests has ever said, "I'm staying in the blue room," because the blues are slate and gray-blues, accented with bits of yellow and orange.

Another way to moderate color is with detail. In my dining room, the deep blue of the walls might dominate the room without the reflective nail heads and the white trim. The tailored feeling of the room, though the room is sparely furnished, gives the eye something to look at. Color becomes just another layer.

Color should never be the point of a room, especially in a country house. The emphasis should always be on what you see outside the window.

Because the main activity in the sunroom is feet-up, stretched-out relaxation, the furniture needed to feel great and to be able to withstand significant wear. Leather, chambray, and wool blends fit the bill.

DOWNSTAIRS GUEST ROOM
MARSHALL STREET BED • ABSTRACT WALLPAPER
• ROPE LAMPS • WELLINGTON HOUSE THREE-DRAWER CHEST
• SLOCUM HALL END TABLES

OPPOSITE: The guest room on the first floor is designed to be a private retreat, far from the other sleeping quarters and out of the traffic pattern of the rest of the house. It is also situated away from the lake, facing the road. My modern take on the canopy bed defines a room-within-a-room with a sense of containment. On the walls is a grassy pattern that, combined with the dark wood tones, evokes the woods, as well as the bedroom's landlocked location in the house.

This room is the most feminine in the house. The bed is an updated version of the classic, romantic four-poster—only spare and with a strong sense of geometry. The night tables are a curving, feminine shape topped with lamps on whimsical, looping bases made of thick dockworkers' rope—the most masculine side of the nautical theme. Only the energetic, grassy green of the wallpaper gets away with being purely feminine. It's organic and pretty, echoed in the figures of tiny leaves on the curtains.

It's a lot to take in, but I've never believed the cherished notion that a small room should be kept simple. The bed in the guest room is a cube that closely repeats the shape of the room and redoubles the right angles of the windows. The effect is a set of rectangles, one inside the other. The rug is the only one in the house with a distinct geometric pattern that engages the X on the ceiling. The girliness softens these angles, while the organic elements give the room a calm air.

The bathroom that I carved out of the original bedroom also has strict lines, but here the plain, boxy shapes and strong vertical of the vanity also suggest an Arts & Crafts simplicity.

It makes sense that this room should be a bit of a departure, since the downstairs guest room is—and this may be the girliest thing about it—a room of one's own, nestled into a

corner away from the lake and at the end of a hallway. There's less foot traffic back there, and the guest can shut the door and be in her or his own little sanctuary. The guest can also expand the room's privacy by closing a door at either end of its hallway. The guest bedroom then becomes the headquarters of a small suite encompassing one full bath and a half bath (the powder room), and a television room complete with a sectional sofa (the media room). I usually reserve this bedroom for families with small children, so parents can let their kids watch television during a grown-up dinner or tuck them into a make-do bed on the media room's sofa, knowing their space is both quiet and contained.

I think of this room as the most feminine space in the house, with the delicate light green on the walls, the pink in the dog portrait, and the lamps with their fun, curvy bases made of rope. However, the dark woods and the solid, almost industrial seriousness of the bathroom fixtures also skew to the masculine.

POWDER ROOM
COPAKE EAGLE CONSOLE • BUTTERFLY WALLPAPER • FRAMED INSECT PRINTS • ROBINEAU ROAD UPHOLSTERED MIRROR • POLISHED NICKEL SCONCES • SEDGWICK SIDE TABLE • BLACK PORCELAIN SINK

ABOVE: All the design elements in the house come into play in the powder room. OPPOSITE: The powder room is more than a room; it's an experience, if for no other reason than the way the Copake Eagle, making its debut here as a bathroom vanity, fixes his stare on the toilet. On the ceiling are more congenial birds, mixing with butterflies. I never make a conscious effort to include birds in the designs for my houses, but I always do.

I am well known for pulling out all the stops in my powder rooms. The powder room should be a "wow" moment, a gift for people who only come over for a cocktail or only stop by briefly. These drive-by guests should not be denied—they deserve an intense dose of the entire design.

Every architectural element of the house is represented here: the *X* on the ceiling, the dining room's corner boards, and the paneling oriented every which way. With its black and white palette, the round mirror in leather of a nautical blue hue, and the nickel tones, the room is the house in miniature.

Two major themes of the house make the cut, too. Since the lake house is my interpretation of American design, I started with my Copake Eagle console—what is more American than a bald eagle? As with so much of the furniture in the house, this console was inspired by a real-life experience. I was looking out the window at my Copake lake house on a winter day some years ago when an eagle swooped down and broke a hole in the ice. It then flew back around to grab a fish out of the lake. Right away I knew I wanted to make a piece of furniture that commemorated the moment. When I designed the eagle, I didn't want a bird that was idealized or symbolic, but ferocious and life-

like—something straight out of Animal Planet. In the tight dimensions of the powder room, it never fails to create an impression.

Inspired in part by the previous owner's wallpaper decorated with leaping deer, I made the bathroom a little Animal Planet, too, incorporating birds and butterflies flitting across the wallpaper on the ceiling and hanging slightly kooky images of insects that I found in an illustrated book. The colorful prints jump off the black walls, ensuring that people emerge from the powder room with something to talk about.

ABOVE LEFT: Outside the powder room, bookshelves original to the house marry seamlessly with the new paneling surrounding them. LEFT: The soapstone sinktop is the same surface used in the kitchen counters. OPPOSITE: Fauna of the creeping-crawling kind decorate the walls of the powder room, which are remarkably active themselves in the chevron pattern of the paneling and the dynamic treatment of the cornerboards and windows.

MEDIA ROOM
LINCOLN HILL SECTIONAL SOFA • DEWITT COCKTAIL TABLE • LYN ACRES UPHOLSTERED CHEST • OTISCO CHAIR • EASTWOOD SIDE TABLE • RESTORATION HARDWARE TRAIN STATION SWING SCONCES AND FILAMENT PENDANT • GOATSKIN RUGS

OPPOSITE: Materials and organic touches used in the sunroom are reprised in the media room, which is similarly designed as a place to spread out and relax. To re-create a little of the sunroom's boldly graphic hardscape, I gave the walls extra dimension by adding regularly spaced battens. A linen woven wall covering— the same one found in the living room—gives the ceiling corresponding depth. For good measure I installed a deer head similar to the sunroom's.

Off the entrance hall is a small room hidden away from the lake and its abundant natural light. I designated it the media room and planned it as a snug, quiet space where one or a few of us might hole up on rainy days or stay-at-home nights and watch TV or a movie.

The media room's distinctive walls grew directly from the five-plank doors: I wanted to make the connection between the paneling and the doors explicit somewhere. I chose the media room because I felt the walls needed to match the bold texture of the chimney rock, and because the room's size would keep my experiment contained.

I played with dimension and depth, adding battens at intervals to imitate the doors' construction. Placing the battens at the same distance as the doors' vertical breaks made for a dizzyingly regular pattern, so I set the battens a little farther apart. The spacing still relates the walls to the doors without being too literal.

Located at the far end of the house from the sunroom, the media room is the sunroom's decorative companion. The fireplace chimney assigns it the same masculine texture that the logs do in the sunroom. Both rooms are intended for lazing around, feet up, with another person or a sleeping dog within arm's reach. It made sense to incorporate the same sort of elements—

a tweedy herringbone on the sectional, leather on the cocktail table, nail heads, and a trophy deer head. Instead of the nautical-inspired rope lamps on the lakeside of the house, I went with a black metal lamp in the middle of the ceiling's *X*. The swiveling wall sconces evoke both library lamps and work lights. Since less sunshine comes into this space than in the sunroom, I reversed the ratio of white to black on the walls, so that they reflect more light.

The media room's commodiousness exerts a pull its television can't explain. I'm not much of a television watcher during my summer weekends, so I'm surprised at how often I find myself spread out on the sofa, reading or just staring out at the tree canopy above the driveway. It's also a place for impromptu guests to stay, or a spot for someone who wants to chill out during a party.

OPPOSITE: The appearance of the chimney's rough stones gives the room warmth, while the furniture and industrial lighting contribute to its natural masculinity. The artwork around the room lightens the look—as do colorful movie-time snacks.

LANDING AND UPSTAIRS HALL
WAINSCOTING · ROPE HANDRAIL · JUTE RUNNER
· STERLING SILVER SCONCES · LINEN WALL COVERING
· DIAMOND WINDOW · BORODINO CONSOLE

OPPOSITE: Expanding the landing afforded the space to create a fully decorated room midway up the stairs. The landing offers a mental reset before you head to the private areas of the house. This transition is subtly signaled by the frame of molding on the window wall. (An identical one frames the bottom of the stairs.)

The staircase in any house is an important transitional space, connecting as it does the public spaces of the house with the private ones. The decoration should reflect this little journey.

With its one open side, the staircase from the first floor to the landing functions almost like a piece of sculpture with a long serrated edge. Its shape is interesting in itself, and it creates a tall, airy space above the short corridor to the front door. Like a public sculpture, the stairs seem to invite people to hang out. Sitting on a midstair step, you are about eye level to someone standing on the floor; that person might lean an elbow on a step while chatting with you.

Because the staircase is almost an extension of the first floor, I pulled in the jute from the underrug in the living room with a jute runner, adding a narrow binding of colorful stripes to give it more visibility. In the same way, I put wainscoting on the wall to carry the bright white wood of the living room's paneled walls upstairs. The beautiful and necessary handrail is a thick nautical rope strung between circular brackets for a barroom foot rail. Its scale is a pleasure to look at, and the material relates not only to the runner but to the ample amount of rope found around the downstairs. (It's also a load off my mind: for months, while I was deciding what to do for a handrail on the stairs, I

worried that a guest was going to take a header off the open side.)

About halfway up the stairs, however, the mood changes. The wainscoting seems to sink away and is replaced by the same Phillip Jeffries Amalfi Silk linen wall covering used in the living room. At the landing there is the sense of a real room, an elegant space with a high table and silver sconces that are fresh and refined. The window wall has weight and moment. A diamond window admits light from the adjoining guest bedroom, adding architectural interest to the wall.

The truth is that the landing is more sophisticated than what you've left or what comes next. The landing is a place where the design catches its breath before it goes upstairs; it's a palate cleanser that resets your expectations, so the next part of the house feels new.

OPPOSITE: Boats are the first image you see as you turn to come upstairs. To the right of this photograph, part of my series with Soicher-Marin, is the laundry room, above left. As we return from boating, swimming, or just a long day on the road, we can toss our clothes in here before heading for a shower. ABOVE: The rope stair railing evokes a ship's rail.

MASTER BEDROOM
HORIZONTAL PANELING • DIAMOND WINDOW •
NATURAL WOOD POST • BED WITH UPHOLSTERED HEADBOARD
• FOREST PRINT WALLPAPER • FERN PATTERN CURTAINS •
JASPER CRACKLE RUG • ANTIQUE RATTAN CHAIRS
• PEBBLE HILL THREE-DRAWER CHEST

OPPOSITE: I balanced the distinct nautical look of the master bedroom's walls with plenty of references to land—the leafy ferns on the curtains and the cracked earth pattern on the rug. These soft browns, found in the barn post and in the bed's fabric headboard (following pages) not only integrate the bedroom with the earthy richness of the living room below, but also give the space a comforting softness.

I'm addicted to anything that has to do with boats. I grew up mucking around in them, and as an adult I have owned one boat or another since I could afford more than my rent in Manhattan. I'm a little embarrassed to admit that even the secret stash of magazines I keep on the bottom shelf of my nightstand is boat porn—yachting magazines that I comb through as I go off to dreams of cool watercraft.

What I loved about the long, low-ceilinged master bedroom at the lake house is that it reminded me of being inside an antique ship. When I designed the room, I pushed the theme further: I turned the direction of the paneling

ninety degrees to horizontal, so that it resembled the planks of a ship's hull. The windows, set closer to the ceiling than the floor, amplify the feeling that I'm belowdecks, so I left them in place.

I had an ulterior motive: preserving the original window placement allowed me to reuse the window frames. Not only was this cheaper, but since I had replaced the walls and ceiling with new paneling, I needed some element of the original house to lend the new parts authenticity.

The high windows are more private, too. The impulse in any vacation home is to maximize the views, especially if you look over water. But the view out of the house isn't the only consideration—the view into the house should be

OPPOSITE AND ABOVE: As I've done elsewhere in the house, I used artwork and accessories to counteract the master bedroom's classic looks with modern, industrial images, abstraction, and contemporary, utilitarian lighting.

factored in as well. There is a lot of boat traffic on the lake during the summer, and not just kids buzzing past at high speed: there are tourist boats with their rails full of gawkers taking in the houses down the lake. I didn't want to worry about tourists watching me shave or take a shower.

My neighbors along the east side of the lake also warned me that too much sun coming in the windows can be annoying. The late sun is very strong, they told me, and has spoiled many an afternoon nap by filling west-facing bedrooms with cooking heat. The relatively high, smaller windows gave me a view from my bed that is only sky, which again reminded me of waking up in a berth on a boat. There's something very restful about lying in bed and watching the passing clouds.

Anyway, the long room felt light and open as it was. By choosing not to close off the bathroom entirely, I had sacrificed the privacy of the sink area—but really, if you've made it as far as my bedroom, am I going to worry if you catch me shaving in a towel? The toilet room was a separate space with its own door, and the shower was tucked securely behind the short wall, and even that barrier admitted fuzzy light through the oversized diamond window.

The black doors, concealing ample closets, seem to recede against the white environment, creating the feeling of even more length.

Ending that wall was a bit of a puzzle for me. A white wood pillar that matched the paneled walls suited the nautical feeling, but to have a nautical end to that wall felt like a failure of imagination. I wanted something that ended the wall like it was a full sentence. Then one day I was at a store that sold reclaimed building materials and found an old barn post, full of local character and an organic, faded softness. It provides a transition to the bathroom that feels peaceful and natural. The person who had built the house using reclaimed barn joists to hold up the living room ceiling would have liked that idea, I think.

Still, the post was the only unpainted wood in the room, and by far the only thing remotely its age. To integrate the barn post into the room, I upholstered my Century Club bed in a velvet fabric the same faun color as the wood. I continued with a rug based on cracked, dry earth, and curtains that are a black, stitched fern pattern, an easy backdrop that matches the forest feeling of the stone octagonals on the shower floor.

The curtains give the room a little bit of softness, and their pattern goes with any bedding. That's important to me, because I like to change the bedding a lot. In the guest rooms, I chose bolder fabrics for my curtains because I can get away with using one or two sets of sheets that I've bought to coordinate with them. The guests aren't around long enough to get sick of their sheets. In my room I usually have six sets, all in different designs, because I want to change them with the seasons.

PAGES 190–191: The organic form of the table lamp matches the barn post's natural grain. PREVIOUS PAGES: Birds make a reappearance in the water closet, around the corner from the decidedly nautical sink area. OPPOSITE: The glassed-in shower, with light entering from three sides, is the next best thing to an outdoor version. The tile on the floor imitates the variegated but closely matched colors of pebbles in a stream, amplifying the feeling of showering outdoors.

UPSTAIRS GUEST ROOM

WOVEN WALLPAPER • STRIPED CURTAINS • MATTYDALE QUEEN BED • ENDERS ROAD LAMP TABLES • RUGBY ROAD CABINET

If the downstairs guest room is feminine, this room is a man in old-school business attire. The slightly shiny gray fabric on the wall recalls a suit, while the striped upholstery on the bed, also used as curtain fabric, is the coordinated dress shirt. The end tables are clean lined and crisply masculine. Even the bathroom, with its classic pedestal sink, coach lanterns, and slim, chrome-framed mirror, has a handsome, no-nonsense feeling. (I briefly considered putting a small sauna in this bathroom to complete the manly spa sensibility, but opted instead for more storage.) As with any room where the fireplace's raw rock is reprised—a piece of the chimney makes up part of the interior wall here—the rough texture of the stone almost demands rugged decor. This aesthetic is

OPPOSITE: Color plays a strong role in the upstairs guest room, with modern greens and subtle gray-blues combining to produce the understated look of men's fashion—fitting for a room with a masculine, tailored feel.

ABOVE AND RIGHT: The size of this bedroom makes it ideal for guests staying for longer periods, and for use as my office while I'm in Skaneateles. It is duly outfitted with a desk and a comfortable spot to read or conduct business by phone.

moderated only by the paneling that shares the wall with the chimney, which both softens and frames the stone.

The longer I stay in Skaneateles, the more projects I get offered in central New York, and the more I find myself at the house alone—and working. When there is no one else around, the guest room doubles as my office away from the office. The simple white desk is as convenient for me as it is for my guests. In the closet off the bathroom I keep supplies, along with my fax, printer, and other equipment.

The re-emergence of the fireplace's stone prompted the addition of a few insects and other allusions to the natural world. The Greek Peak chair, in masculine black with a woven leather seat, ties the guest room to the equally tailored dining room. OPPOSITE: The Rugby Road cabinet's fabric front adds more texture to the room.

OPPOSITE: The bed's skirt stripes reappear in the guest room's bath, complementing the masculine midcentury feel of the fixtures, above. The lanterns on either side of the mirror reprise the living room's lights here.

< 6 >

LETTING A HOUSE
BE A HOME

BY THE SHORELINE ON THE NORTH SIDE OF MY PROPERTY WAS AN old, tumbledown outbuilding that I replaced with a shed we call the boathouse, though it's too small to house any boats. It's a place to stow equipment and the lawn furniture we put on the dock in the summer. Amid the life preservers and extra oars that clutter the boathouse floor, I also keep a box of candles. They are there for summer evenings when we don't want to come inside for the night quite yet. Greg and I will make up a couple of drinks and drag out chairs and sit in the candles' glow and talk. After a weekend of dinner parties and zipping around the lake on my boat, these candlelit chats outside the little shingled shack can feel like the most elegant and sophisticated moments of our stay.

In the end, the lifestyle you create for your house is the final piece of the decor. How you use your house—or, more accurately, *that* you use it—is what gives your home a soul. All the time and effort spent collecting and purchasing is just the beginning. The design is in the living.

In that spirit, I apply the same principles to entertaining as I do to my decor. First, I keep things simple, local, and casual, with enough

The boathouse is an extension of the main house during the summer. Designed to store supplies for outings on the lake and gatherings on the dock, it's also the perfect place to end a long summer weekend.

hints of glamour to make my guests feel something special is in store. If I'm expecting a crowd, I'll set out paper-bag candle lanterns along the front walk. The low light not only feels welcoming and celebratory but also helps guests find their way from the parking area in the dark. Greeting them at the door, I get them a drink and make introductions. After that I leave them to find the food, which I've strategically placed to tell them where to go.

My food, too, is in tune with the atmosphere I want to create. A strange custom has developed in modern entertaining: hosts pester their guests about the food they serve; for example,

by announcing the ingredients of crab-infused appetizers. Greg and I rarely serve appetizers we have to assemble or explain. I buy beautiful olives and interesting-looking salami from the grocery store and put my energy into how I present them.

Another odd modern habit is stripping visitors of their shoes at the door to our homes, a practice that seems to elevate housekeeping over the comfort of our guests. Let people wear their shoes, I say. Floors are meant to be walked on, fabrics are meant to be sat on. The patina of use and age can only be acquired by welcoming

The deck mirrors the living room just on the other side of the bank of windows, with the same sense of symmetry and comfortable ease. Tables positioned just outside the dining room and sunroom can be easily called into use for alfresco meals.

family and friends to come as they are, inviting children to play inside and out, and letting pets on the furniture. Don't save the expensive china for special occasions; use the good stuff for everyday meals. Some of the most beautiful houses in the world are stained and dinged. Their beauty comes in part from the fact that they are reflections of their hosts' outlook of generosity and abundance.

There is a difference between being a laissez-faire host and ignoring your duties. Preparing for a party means anticipating guests' needs and wants. Always have nonalcoholic drinks, especially if children are expected. (This can be as simple as soda or as extravagant as a pitcher of kid cocktails made with cranberry juice, a clear soda, and maraschino cherries.) Know what your friends drink and put it out. I place small silver cups filled with cigarettes at several locations around the party to let people know that they can smoke if they wish. For those who feel they need to sneak a smoke, it's a luxury to have a green light. Outside, Pendleton blankets are on hand in case anyone gets cold.

I give my overnight guests the same personal attention. Next to their beds I put bottles of water and a small dish of ibuprofen. They are provisioned with maps, magazines, and books, robes and toothpaste and plenty of nice towels. Whether they need all of it or not, these comforts draw a picture of the lifestyle I imagined for the house.

It's a lifestyle in which the times are memorable and special. It says we know ourselves to be lucky to be able to live here.

This attitude begins with the renovation itself. The journey has been a long one for me—longer than I expected when I drove up the driveway more than three years ago. The most useful advice I can give anyone embarking on a renovation is to try to enjoy the process of collaborating with all the different professionals. Be conscious that it's a privilege to be able to work with the talented people you meet during the designing and building phase. There are so many pieces of the puzzle that can go wrong; the measure of success is as much how you handle the bad days as the solutions you end up with. How you feel about the work will set the tone for how you'll feel about your house.

PREVIOUS PAGES: The dock is the primary entertainment area on hot summer days, as guests alternately nibble, chat, and jump in for a swim. After sunset, the fire pit becomes the center of action.

EPILOGUE

Late in the summer of 2011, the Skaneateles Historical Society asked me to open my house to the public for a benefit to restore the old Creamery building in town. Hosting a party for the historical society was an honor. It signaled that they felt I'd respected the history of the town, the house, and its surroundings in my renovation. At the same time, it was a little ironic, because I had never intended to pickle the house in period detail. I had always meant to take the house forward, to make it relevant for how we live now, to give it the gift of being an active house again.

But I happily agreed and helped organize the party. We ate food furnished by Doug's Fish Fry and drank local wine, including Anyela's from across the lake, and everything from weekends at posh resorts to turkeys from a farm up

the road was auctioned off. My architect, Bob Eggleston, who was working on the Creamery project, attended, as did a member of the family who owned my house before I did. I remembered how I'd spotted the house after leaving a benefit not unlike this one, and suddenly it seemed as though this great afternoon brought me full circle.

While I always tried during my renovation to respect the design principles that gave my house its grace and proportion, I had also been unafraid to approach the project with my own creativity, or to grant myself license to transform the house so that it became a living, breathing thing. Out of that process will come a new American style that takes the best of traditional design and keeps it alive. It will reimagine our old places and make them home.

ACKNOWLEDGMENTS

My first thanks go to Marc Szafran for his unconditional support, Sabine Rothman, and my brother, Jules, for helping me put together the concept for this book. Thanks to David Vigliano, my literary agent, and to Jennifer Grega and Bob Myman, my attorneys, for their continued support. Thanks go to the entire team at Clarkson Potter, including Doris Cooper, Pam Krauss, Stephanie Huntwork, Kim Tyner, Mark McCauslin, Ashley Phillips, Angelin Borsics, Sean Boyles, and Carly Gorga, for believing in the idea, especially Aliza Fogelson, my patient and always professional editor, who worked so diligently to make it happen. Many thanks to Paul O'Donnell for helping me to get my thoughts down on paper. This book would not be the beautiful thing it is without the amazing dedication of Eric Piasecki, the photographer who allowed me to see my house anew through his eyes. Thanks too to Raina Kattelson, our stylist, and to Zach DeSart for supplemental shots.

My admiration and gratitude to David Lee, Alan Coffin, Jimmy Splane, David's wife, Anne, and the entire crew at David Lee & Co., and to Bob Eggleston, indispensable as an architect and an ally. Thanks to Howard Fisher, Morgan Moss and his crew for their hard work, and Erin Sammut, the Go-To Girl, for being there and doing that, always at the drop of a hat.

Among the many at Thom Filicia Inc. who had a part in this project, I owe a particular debt to Aaron Schurgin for his support, creativity, and expertise, and to Laura Beck for coordinating the many moving parts that went into this book.

A special thanks to the companies and suppliers who graciously extended themselves to be a part of this project and really made it possible: Viking, Eagle Windows and Doors, Sun Valley Bronze, Phillip Jeffries, Pittsburgh Paints, Waterworks, Lutron, Amana, Bosch, Kohler, Restoration Hardware, Waterworks, Conrad Shades, Sacco Carpet, Lumber Liquidators, Historic Housefitters, Vanguard, Kravet, Safavieh, Soicher-Marin, and Classical Elements, all of whom made the process of renovating and decorating my beloved retreat a joy.

Kind thanks to those local professionals whose services made producing the house and book alike a pleasure: Michael Brennan, Kevin Bedenbaugh, Vic Vallar of Vallar's Tile & Marble, Tom Posecznick, Randy Stivers, Becky Nueman, Tom Corona, the team at Ace Fence and Décor Window Fashions, the Sherwood Inn, and the Sailboat Shop for taking care of Tippy. For his friendship and support, I want to thank Ronald Wells at Wells Gallery.

As ever, my appreciation for Greg, who kept us all well fed.

Not least, I extend my thanks to my dad and Laura, David Miller at the Skaneateles Historical Society, and all my fabulous friends and wonderful neighbors. It's the people who make a house a home.

RESOURCES

My renovation was guided by some basic values I'd recommend to anyone trying to breathe life into an old house: affordability, durability, and proportion. In furnishing the house, I was looking for components that fit the spirit of comfort and simple pleasures that inspired the original owners. I wasn't looking to impress anybody with my kitchen equipment or my double doors; I wanted things that were appropriate to the house and its history.

As the renovation went along, as I've described in this book, I increasingly took cues from other recent lifestyle trends that comple- mented my agenda: local sourcing, repurpos- ing our architectural legacy, and preserving regional character. Nobody who worked on the house itself came from more than an hour's drive, and whenever possible I used products from American companies—particularly those that pay attention to craftsmanship and that display respect for American design and the health of our environment (and the dogs and people occupying my house). Regardless of where a manufacturer was located, I looked for products that shared my sensibility of modern design based in traditional values.

SYSTEMS

Amana (heating and air- conditioning): A company with a long history that keeps turning out innovative, high-quality, and energy- efficient products. **amana-hac.com**

Bosch (tankless, on-demand water heater): A market leader in home appliances thanks to their innovative, efficient products. **bosch-climate.us**

Lutron (light switches): I can tell on sight whether it's a Lutron—the look, the finish, and the seamless fit. Their products set the modern standard for lighting and electrical. **lutron.com**

NSC Technologies (Internet and media): Tom Corona wired the old house so that the wireless web and the music and television feeds are completely unobstrusive. **ncstechnologies.net**

APPLIANCES

Viking (stove/oven, refrigerator/ freezer, dishwasher, ice maker, wine fridge): The proven leader in kitchen appliances makes beautifully rugged and precise kitchen equipment. **vikingrange.com**

WINDOWS, LIGHTING, AND HARDWARE

Classical Elements (curtain hardware): A superb resource for window treatment trim and hardware, with accessible products, great price points and people who make everything easy. Check out the Thom Filicia Curtain Hardware Line—a beautiful collaboration between wood and metal. **classicalelements.com**

Eagle (windows): A smart newcomer to the high end, with great design options to give windows a custom look, plus terrific functionality. **eaglewindow.com**

Kohler (faucets and bath fixtures): Marrying great style with accessibility, this global company from a small Wisconsin town is really what we mean when we say "democratic design." An amazing resource with quality products and superb customer service. **kohler.com**

Lumber Liquidators (flooring): The workhorse of American lumber suppliers: fabulous product, great service, and unbeatable price points. **lumberliquidators.comPPG**

Pittsburgh Paint (interior and exterior paint): Incredible color palettes that provided me with plenty of historically correct—and environmentally friendly—options. **pittsburghpaints.com**

Restoration Hardware (light fixtures): A stylish and well-rounded collection of everything from lighting to drawer pulls. **restorationhardware.com**

Sun Valley Bronze (exterior door hardware): Doubly dependable, for their rugged elegance and for their durable, never-fail mechanics. **svbronze.com**

Conrad Shades (handwoven window shades): Their unique and beautiful use of natural materials puts them far ahead of any other company in their category. **conradshades.com**

Kravet (fabrics): A company with an encyclopedic collection of fabrics rooted in the traditional design, and at the same time a cutting-edge company that always has its finger on the pulse of what's happening in the world of textiles. Check out the Thom Filicia Home Collection at **kravet.com**

Phillip Jeffries (wall covering): Beautiful, natural designs that are the benchmark for quality in textured wall coverings. **phillipjeffries.com**

Sacco Carpet (stair runner): A premier source focused on supplying a superior product using sustainable methods, and my go-to for custom carpet and rugs. **saccocarpet.com**

Safavieh (rugs): These rugs are a great balance of modern and classic beauty, with a commitment to quality and affordability that is unparalleled. Check out the Thom Filicia Home Collection at **safavieh.com**

Soicher Marin (artwork): With a voluminous collection, amazingly varied and smart pieces, they are the creative force in the commercial art world today. Check out the Thom Filicia Home Collection at **soicher-marin.com**

Vallar's Tile & Marble (kitchen, bar, and bath counters): Vic Vallar has an encyclopedic knowledge of stone, from exotic to traditional. He's also a master craftsman and a great guy. **vallarsny.com**

Vanguard (furniture): A family-run company committed to American craftsmanship and the highest standards of design and environmentally thoughtful manufacturing. Check out the Thom Filicia Home Collection at **vanguardfurniture.com**

Waterworks (kitchen tile, bar tile, bath tiles, bath stone surrounds, and stone shower saddles): Sophisticated luxury products for the bath and kitchen, from tile to towels, all made with an artisan's sensibility. **waterworks.com**

SERVICES

Ace Fence (fence): A wonderful local resource for fencing and a fabulous team to work with. **acefenceinstalls.com**

David Lee & Company (general contractor): A solutions-oriented builder who delivers high-quality, beautifully detailed results as if he were working on his own house. **dleeco.com**

Décor Window Fashions: A great workroom, beautiful details, fabulous installers. 315-474-5044

The Go-To Girl, Erin Sammut (concierge services): Simply the best at doing all of those little things here and there with a great deal of care and an eye for the details. A lot of fun and a wonderful friend. **thego-togirlconcierge.com**

Michael Brennan (landscaping): Michael magically transformed the yard overnight from a construction site to the foundation of a beautifully landscaped property. I love his enthusiasm, professionalism, and creativity. **pagodahill@yahoo.com**

Robert O. Eggleston (architect): Accomplished, expert design that puts the clients' goals and wishes first. 315-685-8144

Rebecca Nueman (painting and wallpapering): Becky immediately took to the spirit of the house, and finished the walls with caring efficiency. 315-243-6633

Tim Posecznick (property management): Tim is a great guy and a wonderful local resource who can do it all, from lawn care to beautifully stacked wood, installation of dock to a stacked stone fire pit. **orchardslopefarm@hotmail.com**

Sailboat Shop (boat care and maintenance): John at the Sailboat Shop continues to take the best of care of Tippy, my trusty lake steed. 315-685-7558

Sebastian Wintermute Restoration & Preservation (photography restoration): Works modern-tech magic on vintage documents and photographs. **sebastianwintermute.com**

Stivers Upholstery (nailhead details): Quick, precise, and a pleasure to work with, Stivers is another small Syracuse company with the professionalism of a national brand. 315-455-1175